make mine

Low-Fat

and tasty, too!

LF5016

Printed in the USA

ISBN #0-934474-72-9

25 Healthy and Low-Fat Tips

- Prepare a grocery list and stick to it while shopping—your waistline and pocketbook will both thank you.

- Do your grocery shopping on a full stomach—hunger can lead to impulsive buying.

- To save calories, try lightly dipping your pancakes, waffles, or French toast into syrup rather than pouring the syrup over the top of them.

- Eating an egg for breakfast every other morning instead of every morning for one year saves the same amount of fat as in a 32 ounce bottle of oil.

- Switching from whole milk to skim milk, assuming you drink 2 cups per day, will save the same amount of fat as in 29 sticks of butter over a one year time period.

- Many people say they do not have time to exercise, but will wait for an elevator instead of taking the stairs or will circle the parking lot until a close parking space opens.

- Walking is an easy and inexpensive way to get aerobic exercise—20 minutes or more of brisk walking each day is a great way to get in shape and stay that way.

- Eat the potatoes or the pastas; skip the butter, sour cream, cream sauce, or gravy on the top.

- Your taste buds will be much more accepting of a gradual decrease in salt rather than cutting out salt "cold turkey."

- For low-fat meat preparation, remember the four B's: Bake, Broil, Boil, or Barbecue.

- Do not worry about an occasional indulgence on a high calorie and/or high fat food; focus instead on improving daily eating habits.

- Skipping breakfast may make it harder to take off pounds, not easier.

- Vitamin C improves the absorption of iron and calcium. If you take a multiple vitamin and mineral supplement, take it with your morning glass of orange juice.

- Avoid the "fast cure" for weight loss—gradual changes in diet and lifestyle are more likely to become permanent changes.

- Red meats, such as beef and pork, can be part of a healthy diet; just eat them in moderation and choose low-fat cuts with excess fat trimmed away.

- Try cooking meats on a wire rack to allow the fat to drain off. Non-stick cookware and vegetable oil spray help to reduce the amount of fat needed for cooking.

- Cook ground beef until it is no longer pink to be sure harmful bacteria are killed.

- Be cautious of fad diets or diet supplements with unproven medical claims. In most cases, the saying, "If it sounds too good to be true, it probably is," rings true.

- By eating a variety of foods each day, most people can get adequate amounts of vitamins and minerals without taking supplements.

- Restaurant dining does not have to mean a high fat meal. Choose entrees that are broiled or baked rather than fried. Ask for sauces, dressings, and condiments on the side so you can better control how much of these you eat.

- When checking a list of ingredients for **sodium,** watch also for terms such as **salt, soda, Na,** and **MSG.** These terms represent sodium containing ingredients.

- Terms used to describe sugars in foods include **sugar, sucrose, glucose, fructose, honey, corn syrup, high-fructose corn syrup, molasses,** and **fruit juice concentrate.**

- When food is allowed to thaw at room temperature, the surface temperature may get warm enough to allow bacteria to grow, even though the middle of the food is still frozen.

- Margarine may not have any cholesterol, but it has the same amount of fat in it as butter. It, too, needs to be eaten in moderation.

- Choose low-fat snacks such as pretzels, low-fat popcorn, fat free crackers, frozen yogurt, sherbet, or low-fat ice cream instead of chips, dips, nuts, and regular ice cream.

TABLE OF CONTENTS

APPETIZERS, BEVERAGES 1

SOUPS, SALADS 7

VEGETABLES 21

MAIN DISHES 31

BREADS, ROLLS 55

DESSERTS 61

MISCELLANEOUS 77

LF5016

FAVORITE RECIPES
FROM MY COOKBOOK

Recipe Name	Page Number

APPETIZERS, BEVERAGES

COTTAGE CHEESE SPREAD

1 (12 oz.) container 1%
  low-fat cottage cheese
1 tsp. dried whole
  summer savory
½ c. diced tomato,
  drained
⅓ c. shredded carrot
⅓ c. chopped unpeeled
  cucumber
⅓ c. chopped green
  pepper
¼ c. sliced green onions
1 Tbsp. red wine vinegar

Combine cottage cheese and savory; stir well. Add remaining ingredients; toss gently. Cover and chill. Makes 4 servings.

Note: Suggested bases for sandwich filling include flatbreads, crisp breads, cracker breads, and rice cakes.

Per serving:
Calories: 77
Fat: 1 gram
Percentage of calories from fat: 12%

CUCUMBER DILL DIP

1 (16 to 24 oz.) container
  fat-free cottage cheese
¼ c. skim or ½% milk
1 env. reduced calorie fat
  free Ranch salad
  dressing mix
1 medium cucumber,
  peeled, seeded, and
  chopped
2 Tbsp. (or more to taste)
  finely chopped green
  onion
1 tsp. dill weed

Puree cottage cheese with hand mixer or in blender with milk and salad dressing mix. Stir in remaining ingredients. Refrigerate. Serve with vegetable dippers. Makes 3 cups.

You can use Light 'n Lively cottage cheese and Hidden Valley Ranch reduced calorie Original Ranch salad dressing mix. This makes for a low calorie, low sodium, no fat, delicious alternative to vegetable dip. *Enjoy!*

Per serving:
Calories (per 3 tablespoons): 28
Total fat: Less than 1 gram
Percentage of calories from fat: 4%

LAYERED MEXICAN DIP

2 (1 lb.) cans fat-free
    refried beans
½ lb. ground turkey,
    cooked and drained
    (white tenderloin
    skinless)
3 c. nonfat Mozzarella
    cheese
1 c. grated nonfat
    Cheddar cheese
1 (16 oz.) jar taco sauce
4 oz. can chopped green
    chiles
1 c. fat-free sour cream
3 Tbsp. fat-free chicken
    broth
1 large onion, diced

Brown diced onion in chicken broth. Add cooked ground turkey. Stir refried beans into turkey mixture. Spread into a 9x13 inch casserole dish that has been sprayed with a nonfat cooking spray. Sprinkle green chiles over top of turkey-bean mixture. Spread ½ of cheese over this. Pour taco sauce over cheese. Sprinkle remaining cheese on top and bake at 400°F. for 20 to 25 minutes. Cool slightly and spoon sour cream to make a cross on top of casserole. Serve with low-fat tortilla chips or homemade low-fat chips. Makes 32 servings.

Per serving:
Calories: 72
Fat: Less than 1 gram
Percentage of calories from fat: 1%

PINEAPPLE-APRICOT SPREAD

¾ c. chopped dried
    apricots (16 apricot
    halves)
1 c. pineapple juice
2 Tbsp. firmly packed
    brown sugar
1/16 tsp. ground cinnamon

In a blender container, combine all ingredients. Blend until apricots are finely chopped. Pour mixture into a small saucepan. Bring to a boil over medium heat, stirring occasionally. Reduce heat to low and cook 20 minutes, stirring frequently. Serve warm or spoon into a small bowl or jar and chill. Serve on bread or crackers and even doubles as a topping for low fat ice cream. Makes 6 servings.

Per serving:
Calories: 68
Fat: Less than 1 gram
Percentage of calories from fat: 1%

VEGETABLE DIP

½ c. nonfat plain yogurt
¼ tsp. dill weed
1 tsp. minced onion
½ packet artificial
    sweetener
Raw vegetables (serve
    with)

Mix all ingredients thoroughly. Chill several hours. Serve with raw crisp vegetables. Makes 8 servings.

Per serving:
Calories: 8
Fat: 0 grams
Percentage of calories from fat: 0%

CHEESY PIZZA SNACKS

¼ c. low-fat Ricotta
  cheese
¼ tsp. Italian seasoning
1 clove garlic, crushed
8 rye-crisp crackers (any
  flavor)
2 Tbsp. shredded
  Mozzarella cheese
1½ Tbsp. freshly
  shredded Parmesan
  cheese
1 roma (plum) tomato,
  thinly sliced and cut in
  half, or ¼ c. spaghetti
  sauce*
Dash of pepper

Heat oven to 375°. Mix Ricotta cheese, Italian seasoning, and garlic; spread on crackers. Sprinkle with Mozzarella and Parmesan cheeses. Arrange 2 tomato slices on each cracker. Sprinkle with pepper. Place crackers on ungreased cookie sheet. Bake 9 to 11 minutes or until cheese is melted and begins to turn golden brown. Makes 8 servings.

* If using spaghetti sauce, spread over Ricotta mixture before sprinkling with cheeses.

Per serving:
Calories: 47
Fat: 1 gram
Percentage of calories from fat: 17%

CRAB TOAST APPETIZERS

8 oz. lump crabmeat
½ c. diced red pepper
2 Tbsp. plus 2 tsp.
  reduced calorie
  mayonnaise
2 Tbsp. chopped fresh
  parsley
1 Tbsp. chopped fresh
  chives
1 Tbsp. fresh lime juice
1 Tbsp. Dijon mustard
2 tsp. grated Parmesan
  cheese
4 to 5 drops of hot pepper
  sauce
4 oz. Italian bread, cut
  into 16 slices

Preheat the broiler; line broiler pan with foil. Pick over crabmeat to remove any cartilage. In medium bowl, combine crabmeat, bell pepper, mayonnaise, parsley, chives, lime juice, mustard, cheese, and hot pepper sauce; blend well. Spread 1 tablespoon of crab mixture on each slice of bread. Place bread on the broiler pan and broil 4 inches from the heat for 5 to 6 minutes or until lightly browned. Makes 8 servings.

Per serving:
Calories: 86
Fat: 2 grams
Percentage of calories from fat: 24%

GRANOLA

6 c. old-fashioned oats
1½ tsp. cinnamon
1 tsp. nutmeg
1 Tbsp. vanilla
¼ c. canola oil
¼ c. honey
½ c. raisins

Mix oil, honey, and raisins. In large bowl, mix rest of ingredients and pour oil mixture over; stir to mix. Put on large cookie sheet with rim. Spread out even. Bake 2 hours at 250°, stirring every 20 minutes. Makes 6½ cups. Makes 13 servings.

Per serving:
Calories: 216
Fat: 7 grams
Percentage of calories from fat: 29%

POTATO SKINS

6 medium russet potatoes
½ c. shredded nonfat
   Cheddar cheese
1 pkg. butter substitute,
   mixed with hot water
⅔ c. green onions,
   chopped
⅛ c. imitation bacon
   pieces
Salsa
Nonfat sour cream

Bake potatoes and cool completely. When potatoes are cool enough to handle, slice them open and scoop out the middle. Be sure to leave enough potato to keep the shell firm and standing. Combine butter substitute, onions, and bacon pieces. Divide evenly between 12 potato halves; sprinkle with cheese and bake for 5 to 6 minutes at 425°. Top with salsa or sour cream or other favorite toppings. Makes 12 servings.

Per serving:
Calories: 48
Fat: Less than 1 gram
Percentage of calories from fat: 4%

SCALLOP AND HAM ROLL-UPS

24 sea scallops (about ¾
   lb.)
6 oz. thinly sliced lean
   ham, visible fat
   removed
24 pineapple chunks
   (canned in their own
   juice, about ½ of a 20
   oz. can)
24 toothpicks, soaked in
   water for at least 30
   minutes

Preheat broiler. If the muscle is still attached to the scallop, remove it. Cut ham into approximately 6 x 1¼ inch strips. Wrap one strip around each scallop and skewer with a toothpick. Add 1 pineapple chunk to each toothpick. Place prepared toothpicks on a baking pan with sides. Broil 5 inches from heat for 4 minutes. Turn scallops and broil another 3 minutes. Serve hot. Makes 12 servings.

Per serving:
Calories: 52
Fat: 1 gram
Percentage of calories from fat: 26%

TURKEY MEATBALLS

1 lb. lean ground white
   meat skinless turkey
½ c. crushed fat free
   wheat crackers
¼ chopped onion
1 egg substitute (¼ c.)
1 Tbsp. chicken broth
1 Tbsp. Worcestershire
   sauce
¼ tsp. lite salt (optional)
½ tsp. poultry seasoning

Spicy Sauce:
½ c. chile sauce
2 Tbsp. vinegar
2 Tbsp. brown sugar

Mix all of the ingredients together and roll into bite-size balls. Place meatballs on top of a broiler pan so any fat will fall through. Bake at 375°F. for about 15 to 20 minutes. Makes 10 servings (5 balls each).

Spicy Sauce: Use as a dip for meatballs.

Per serving:
Calories: 96
Fat: Less than 1 gram
Percentage of calories from fat: 4%

BANANA SMOOTHIE

1 c. orange or pineapple
   juice
1 banana, sliced
½ c. plain nonfat yogurt
3 ice cubes or 3 large
   frozen strawberries

Combine all ingredients in a blender or food processor. Blend until smooth. Makes 1 serving.

Per serving:
Calories: 286
Fat: 2 grams
Percentage of calories from fat: 5%

CRAN-BANANA COOLER

2 c. cranberry juice
   cocktail, chilled
1 c. milk
1 c. vanilla ice cream
2 Tbsp. honey
2 bananas, cut into pieces

In blender container, combine all ingredients. Cover; blend until smooth. Makes 5 servings.

Per serving:
Calories: 188
Fat: 3 grams
Percentage of calories from fat: 13%

ORANGE-STRAWBERRY JUICE FROTH

2 c. orange juice
1½ c. apricot nectar
1 c. frozen sweetened
   strawberries

In blender, process ingredients for about 20 seconds, or until smooth and frothy. Serve immediately. Makes 6 servings.

Per serving:
Calories: 105
Fat: Less than 1 gram
Percentage of calories from fat: 3%

RASPBERRY COOLER

¼ c. sugar
½ c. mint leaves
1 c. water
1 (10 oz.) pkg. frozen
  raspberries
1 (6 oz.) can frozen
  limeade or lemonade
  concentrate
2 c. club soda

Combine sugar, leaves, and water in 2 quart casserole. Cook on FULL power for 2½ to 4 minutes or until mixture boils. Stir halfway through cooking time. Let stand for 5 minutes. Add frozen raspberries and limeade; stir in club soda just before serving. Serve on ice. Makes 8 servings.

Per serving:
Calories: 102
Fat: Less than 1 gram
Percentage of calories from fat: 1%

TUTTI-FRUTTI COOLER

4 (6½ oz.) bottles
  sparkling mineral
  water, chilled
2 (12 oz.) cans peach
  nectar, chilled
1 c. unsweetened orange
  juice, chilled
½ c. unsweetened
  grapefruit juice, chilled
¼ c. lemon juice, chilled
Orange rind strips

Combine all ingredients in a large pitcher; mix well. Pour over ice cubes in serving glasses; garnish with strips of orange rind. Makes 8 servings.

Per serving:
Calories: 72
Fat: Less than 1 gram
Percentage of calories from fat: 1%

YOGURT SHAKE

3 c. cold low-fat milk
1 (4 serving size) pkg.
  sugar free instant
  pudding and pie filling
  (any flavor)
1 (8 oz.) container plain
  low-fat yogurt
1 c. crushed ice
1 medium banana, cut
  into chunks*

Combine all ingredients in blender in order given; cover. Blend at high speed for 1 minute. Pour into glasses. Serve immediately. Makes 9 servings.

* You may substitute ½ cup sliced strawberries for banana chunks.

Per serving:
Calories: 67
Fat: 1 gram
Percentage of calories from fat: 7%

SOUPS, SALADS

ALL-OCCASION SOUP

1 (16 oz.) can tomatoes,
  crushed
2 cans water
1 onion, diced
4 stalks celery, diced
2 chicken bouillon cubes
20 oz. frozen green beans
16 to 20 oz. frozen sliced
  carrots
1 small head cabbage,
  chopped
Italian seasoning to taste
  (garlic powder,
  oregano, basil)

Add all ingredients to large pot. Cover and simmer 1½ hours. Puree 1½ blender containers and add to rest of soup. May be frozen. Makes 6 servings.

Per serving:
Calories: 128
Fat: 1 gram
Percentage of calories from fat: 7%

BEAN AND CABBAGE SOUP

4 c. no-salt-added beef
  broth
1 head cabbage (1½ lb.),
  coarsely chopped (8 c.)
1½ c. sliced carrots
1 c. sliced onions
½ tsp. ground allspice
1 (19 oz.) can white
  kidney beans, rinsed
  and drained
½ c. chopped fresh dill or
  2 Tbsp. dried dill weed
Light sour cream and
  fresh dill (optional)

In large saucepan, bring broth, 1 cup water, cabbage, carrots, onion, and allspice to a boil. Reduce heat, cover, and simmer 12 minutes, or until vegetables are firm-tender.

Add beans and dill; simmer, uncovered, 5 minutes. Garnish with sour cream and dill. Makes 4 servings.

Per serving:
Calories: 173
Fat: 2 grams
Percentage of calories from fat: 8%

BEAN AND MACARONI STEW

1 c. coarsely chopped
   tomato (about 1 large)
¾ c. uncooked medium
   macaroni shells
¼ c. chopped onion
   (about 1 small)
¼ c. chopped green bell
   pepper
1¾ c. vegetable stock
1 Tbsp. chopped fresh or
  1 tsp. dried basil leaves
1 tsp. Worcestershire
   sauce
1 clove garlic, finely
   chopped
1 (16 oz.) can kidney
   beans, drained
½ (15 oz.) can garbanzo
   beans, drained

Mix all ingredients in 2 quart saucepan. Heat to boiling, stirring occasionally. Reduce heat. Cover and simmer about 15 minutes, stirring occasionally, until pasta is tender. Makes 4 servings.

Per serving:
Calories: 212
Fat: 2 grams
Percentage of calories from fat: 7%

BEAN 'N' GREENS SOUP

1 tsp. olive oil
½ c. chopped onion
2 cloves garlic, minced
2 (15 oz.) cans garbanzo
   beans
5 c. salt-free chicken
   broth, defatted
1 pkg. frozen chopped
   spinach, mustard
   greens *or* Swiss chard,
   thawed and drained
1 c. cooked small pasta
   shells *or* ½ c. cooked
   brown rice
1 tsp. lite salt

Heat olive oil in a skillet; saute onion and garlic until soft. Set aside. Puree 1 can of beans. Combine with remaining ingredients, including onion and garlic. Simmer 30 minutes. Makes 8 servings.

Per serving:
Calories: 143
Fat: 2 grams
Percentage of calories from fat: 14%

QUICK BEAN-ROTINI SOUP

1 medium onion, sliced
2 cloves garlic, crushed
4 oz. fully cooked smoked ham, chopped (about 1 c.)
1 (16 oz.) can whole tomatoes (undrained)
3 c. water
1 tsp. dried oregano leaves
½ tsp. dried thyme leaves
¼ tsp. pepper
1 c. uncooked spiral macaroni
2 medium potatoes, cut into ½ inch pieces
1 (20 oz.) can cannellini beans, drained
1 small zucchini, thinly sliced
⅓ c. grated Parmesan cheese (if desired)

Spray 4 quart Dutch oven with nonstick cooking spray. Cook and stir onion, garlic, and ham in Dutch oven over medium heat about 5 minutes or until onion is tender. Stir in tomatoes, water, oregano, thyme, and pepper. Break up tomatoes with fork. Heat to boiling. Stir in macaroni and potatoes; reduce heat. Cook, uncovered, about 10 minutes or until macaroni is tender. Stir in beans and zucchini. Cook about 3 minutes or just until zucchini is crisp-tender. Sprinkle each serving with Parmesan cheese. Makes 6 servings.

Per serving:
Calories: 228
Fat: 4 grams
Percentage of calories from fat: 15%

CHEESY CREAMY BROCCOLI SOUP

1 c. nonfat dry milk
2 c. nonfat milk
1 tsp. olive oil
½ c. chopped onion
2 c. salt-free chicken broth, defatted
2 c. chopped broccoli
¼ c. water
¼ c. unbleached flour
1 c. grated low-fat Cheddar cheese
1 to 2 Tbsp. dry sherry
¼ tsp. white pepper

Blend dry milk into liquid nonfat milk; stir well and set aside. Heat olive oil in a large saucepan. Saute onions until soft, 2 to 3 minutes. Add chicken broth and broccoli. Simmer 10 to 15 minutes or until broccoli is tender.

Blend water into flour and add to soup along with milk mixture, cheese, sherry, and pepper. Bring to a boil, stirring constantly; reduce heat and simmer until thickened. Makes 6 servings.

Variation: Puree cooked broccoli before adding remaining ingredients.

Per serving:
Calories: 204
Fat: 5 grams
Percentage of calories from fat: 23%

CHICKPEA AND BROWN RICE SOUP

1 c. (6½ oz.) dried chickpeas (garbanzo beans), picked over and soaked
1 Tbsp. olive oil
2 c. chopped onions
¾ c. diced celery
2 Tbsp. minced fresh garlic
¾ tsp. fennel or anise seeds
¾ tsp. cumin seeds
4 c. water
3½ c. chicken broth (reduced sodium), fat skimmed
¾ c. raw brown rice
¾ c. chopped parsley
2 Tbsp. fresh squeezed lemon juice
½ tsp. salt (or omit)
¼ tsp. pepper

Rinse and drain soaked chickpeas. Heat oil in a heavy 5 quart pot over medium heat. Add onions, celery, and garlic. Cook about 7 minutes until vegetables are almost tender. Add fennel and cumin seeds. Stir 30 seconds to release flavors and blend.

Add chickpeas, water, broth, and rice. Cover and bring to a boil over high heat. Reduce heat and simmer 1¼ to 1½ hours until chickpeas are tender. Remove from heat and stir in remaining ingredients. Makes 9 (1 cup) servings.

Per serving:
Calories: 175
Fat: 4 grams
Percentage of calories from fat: 17%

CHICKEN BROTH

1 large chicken
3 qt. cold water
2 stalks celery (with leaves)
2 carrots, peeled and chopped
1 large onion, chopped
4 tsp. minced garlic (in a jar)
¼ tsp. basil
4 peppercorns
1 Tbsp. or less lite salt (optional)
⅛ tsp. pepper

Put chicken and water in a stock pot. Cover; simmer 2½ hours or until chicken is tender and away from the bone. Strain. Remove from bones. (Freeze bones for later use.) Refrigerate overnight; fat will float to the top. Skim and discard the fat.

Heat broth to boiling; add vegetables and seasonings. Simmer 2 hours; strain. Reserve vegetables for soup or later use; use broth within 2 weeks or freeze. For a richer broth, add another chicken or additional white meat chicken parts. Makes 16 servings.

Per serving:
Calories: 14
Fat: Less than 1 gram
Percentage of calories from fat: 13%

SOUTHWEST CHICKEN SOUP

1 c. chopped onion
1/2 c. chopped celery
1 Tbsp. olive oil
6 c. chicken stock
4 chicken breast halves
4 chicken thighs
1/2 c. brown rice
1 (10 oz.) pkg. frozen cut
  corn
1 tsp. cumin
1 Tbsp. chili powder
2 Tbsp. picante sauce
1 (15½ oz.) can diced
  tomatoes
1 (4 oz.) can chopped
  green chilies

In a soup kettle, saute the onions and celery in the oil until soft. Add chicken stock, chicken pieces, and brown rice. Bring mixture to a boil. Reduce heat, cover, and simmer until chicken is tender, 20 to 30 minutes. Remove chicken and set aside to cool. Chill until fat hardens. Skim fat off of the top and discard. Remove chicken from the bones and add to the stock along with remaining ingredients. Heat through; adjust seasoning. Makes 8 servings.

Per serving:
Calories: 261
Fat: 5 grams
Percentage of calories from fat: 18%

CORN AND POTATO CHOWDER

1/2 c. water
3 c. frozen whole kernel
  corn, thawed
1 Tbsp. margarine or
  butter
1/4 c. chopped onion
1 garlic clove, minced
2 Tbsp. all-purpose flour
1/2 tsp. dry mustard
1/4 tsp. salt
1/8 to 1/4 tsp. pepper
1 (12 oz.) can evaporated
  skim milk
1½ c. frozen hash brown
  potatoes
2 Tbsp. chopped fresh
  parsley

In blender container or food processor bowl with metal blade, combine water and 2 cups of the corn. Cover; blend at high speed for 1 minute or until smooth. Set aside.

Melt margarine in large saucepan over medium heat. Add onion and garlic; cook until tender. Stir in flour, dry mustard, salt, and pepper. Gradually add milk. Cook, stirring constantly, until thick and bubbly. Stir corn puree, remaining 1 cup corn, hash brown potatoes, and parsley into soup. Cover; cook over low heat for 10 to 15 minutes or until potatoes are tender. If desired, garnish with fresh chopped parsley. Makes 4 (1 cup) servings.

Tip: If soup becomes too thick, add a small amount of water.

Per serving:
Calories: 285
Fat: 5 grams
Percentage of calories from fat: 14%

FRENCH ONION SOUP

5 large yellow onions
¼ tsp. black pepper
1 Tbsp. flour
3 cans nonfat beef broth
3 c. water
1 bay leaf
8 slices French bread
1 c. nonfat shredded
   Mozzarella cheese

Peel onions and slice thin. Spray 4 quart saucepan; add onions and pepper. Saute until onions are a light golden brown; stir frequently. Sprinkle onions with flour and stir until all traces of flour disappear. Cook 1 minute longer, stirring constantly with wooden spoon. Remove from heat.

Gradually add beef broth, stirring onion mixture constantly. Stir in bay leaf and water. Return to moderately high heat and bring mixture to a boil, stirring constantly. Reduce heat to low and cook, uncovered, for 30 to 40 minutes. Discard bay leaf.

Taste; add salt and pepper if desired. Ladle soup into *broilerproof* soup bowls on a jelly roll pan. Toast bread slices in toaster or under broiler until golden brown. Arrange toast slices on top of onion soup and sprinkle with cheese. Place under broiler; broil until cheese melts and turns golden brown. Remove from oven and serve immediately. Makes 8 servings.

Per serving:
Calories: 146
Fat: 1 gram
Percentage of calories from fat: 7%

LENTIL-SAUSAGE SOUP

2 c. no-salt-added
   vegetable juice cocktail
1 c. water
½ c. dry lentils
¼ c. chopped onion
1 garlic clove, minced
½ tsp. dried thyme leaves
Dash of pepper
2 c. frozen mixed
   vegetables
6 frozen fully cooked light
   breakfast sausage links,
   cut into ½ inch slices

In large saucepan, bring vegetable juice cocktail and water to a boil. Stir in lentils, onion, garlic, thyme, and pepper. Reduce heat; cover and simmer 30 to 35 minutes or until lentils are tender. Return to a boil. Add vegetables and sausage. Reduce heat; simmer about 5 minutes or until vegetables are tender. Makes 4 (1¼ cup) servings.

Per serving:
Calories: 225
Fat: 5 grams
Percentage of calories from fat: 18%

MEATBALL SOUP

Meatballs:
1½ lb. ground skinless
   white meat turkey
¼ c. egg substitute
3 Tbsp. water
½ c. dry bread crumbs
¼ tsp. salt
1 Tbsp. chopped parsley

Soup:
2 c. water
1 (10½ oz.) can
   condensed beef broth
   (low sodium and
   undiluted)
1 (1 lb. 12 oz.) can
   tomatoes, chopped (low
   sodium and *undrained*)
1 (1⅜ oz.) env. dry onion
   soup mix
1 c. sliced carrots
¼ c. chopped celery tops
¼ c. chopped parsley
¼ tsp. black pepper
¼ tsp. dried oregano
   leaves
¼ tsp. dried basil leaves
1 bay leaf

To make the meatballs, combine turkey, egg, water, bread crumbs, salt, and parsley. Mix lightly; shape into 24 balls. In 5 quart Dutch oven, brown meatballs, a single layer at a time, on all sides. Drain off fat; remove meatballs and set aside.

To make soup, combine ingredients in same Dutch oven. Bring to boiling. Reduce heat, cover, and simmer for 20 minutes. Add meatballs; simmer 20 minutes longer. Makes 8 servings.

Per serving:
Calories: 178
Fat: 2 grams
Percentage of calories from fat: 8%

QUICK TOMATO BARLEY SOUP

1 (28 oz.) can Italian
   tomatoes
2 (10 oz.) cans salt-free
   chicken broth, defatted
½ c. pearl barley
1 Tbsp. chopped fresh
   basil (*or* ½ tsp. dried)
⅛ tsp. celery seed,
   ground
Dash of allspice

Puree tomatoes in a food processor. Pour into a saucepan and add remaining ingredients. Bring to a boil. Reduce heat and simmer, stirring occasionally, for about 30 minutes or until barley is soft. Makes 6 servings.

Per serving:
Calories: 99
Fat: 1 gram
Percentage of calories from fat: 5%

HOMESTYLE TURKEY SOUP

6 lb. turkey breast
2 medium onions
3 stalks celery
1 tsp. dried thyme
½ tsp. dried rosemary
½ tsp. sage
1 tsp. basil (dried)
½ tsp. marjoram
½ tsp. dried tarragon
½ lb. Italian pastina (or pasta of your choice)
½ tsp. salt
Pepper to taste

Place turkey in 6 quart pot. Cover with water at least ¾ full. Add peeled onions, cut in large pieces. Wash celery; slice and add also. Simmer, covered, for 2½ hours. Remove carcass and cool soup in refrigerator. When cool, skim fat. While soup is cooling, remove meat. Cut in pieces. Add meat to soup with herbs and spices. Bring to boil; add pastina. Continue cooking; low boil 20 minutes till pastina is done. Serve at once or refrigerate and reheat later. Makes 16 (1 cup) servings.

Per serving:
Calories: 212
Fat: 1 gram
Percentage of calories from fat: 4%

TURKEY-BARLEY SOUP

1 lb. ground turkey
⅔ c. uncooked quick-cooking barley
2 (14½ oz.) cans ready-to-serve beef broth
2 (16 oz.) cans whole tomatoes (undrained)
2 c. frozen mixed vegetables

Cook ground turkey in Dutch oven over medium heat, stirring occasionally, until turkey is white; drain. Stir in barley, broth, and tomatoes. Heat to boiling, stirring occasionally; reduce heat. Cover and simmer 15 minutes. Stir in frozen vegetables. Cover and simmer about 10 minutes longer or until barley is tender. Makes 6 servings.

Per serving:
Calories: 282
Fat: 7 grams
Percentage of calories from fat: 23%

CURRIED VEGETABLE SALAD

⅔ c. fat-free plain yogurt
1 Tbsp. chutney
1 tsp. curry powder
½ tsp. salt
2½ c. thinly sliced cucumber (about 2 medium)
1½ c. chopped tomato (about 2 medium)
½ c. chopped green bell pepper (about 1 small)
¼ c. chopped onion (about 1 small)

Mix yogurt, chutney, curry powder, and salt in 3 quart bowl; toss with remaining ingredients. Cover and refrigerate at least 8 hours but no longer than 24 hours. Sprinkle with flaked or shredded coconut if desired. Makes 6 servings.

Per serving:
Calories: 48
Fat: Less than 1 gram
Percentage of calories from fat: 8%

MOCK EGG SALAD SANDWICHES

2 (8 oz.) ctn. egg
 substitute, hard cooked
 and chopped

2 Tbsp. Dijon mustard
½ c. fat-free mayonnaise
 or salad dressing
¼ c. chopped celery
¼ c. chopped red pepper
2 Tbsp. chopped scallions
12 slices white bread
6 lettuce leaves

In a large nonstick skillet, pour egg substitute in and cover tightly, cooking over a very low heat for 10 minutes or until just set. Remove from skillet and cool completely. Chop into fine pieces.

In a bowl, combine hard cooked egg substitute that has been chopped, Dijon mustard, mayonnaise, celery, red peppers, and scallions. Divide and spread on 6 bread slices. Top with lettuce and remaining bread. Serve immediately. Makes 6 servings.

Per serving:
Calories: 238
Fat: 5 grams
Percentage of calories from fat: 18%

SEAFOOD FRUIT SALAD

Chicken Salad:
2 c. cooked chicken or
 turkey, cubed
¼ c. light mayonnaise

1 c. seedless grapes,
 halved (red or green)
1 c. cantaloupe or
 honeydew, drained
1 (8 oz.) can sliced water
 chestnuts, drained
1 (4½ oz.) can shrimp,
 rinsed and drained
1 small banana
1 Tbsp. lemon juice

Mash banana and stir in lemon juice. Cover and chill for several hours. Combine chicken, grapes, melon, water chestnuts, and shrimp in large bowl. Cover and chill several hours. Arrange leaf lettuce on a plate. Serve 6 ounces of salad on top of lettuce. Top with lemon banana dressing. Makes 6 servings.

Per serving:
Calories: 155
Fat: 5 grams
Percentage of calories from fat: 29%

PEA SALAD

⅓ c. plain low-fat yogurt
1½ Tbsp. Dijon mustard
⅛ tsp. ground pepper
1 (10 oz.) pkg. frozen
  petite peas, thawed
1 hard cooked egg,
  chopped
½ c. finely chopped red
  bell pepper
⅓ c. thinly sliced green
  onions (including tops)
¼ c. thinly sliced celery
Lettuce leaves

In a 2 to 3 quart bowl, combine yogurt, mustard, and ground pepper; mix until smooth. Add peas, egg, bell pepper, onions, and celery. Mix lightly to coat vegetables with dressing. Cover and refrigerate for at least 3 hours or until next day.

Line a platter or individual plates with lettuce and spoon salad over. Makes 6 servings.

Per serving:
Calories: 65
Fat: 1 gram
Percentage of calories from fat: 20%

TWENTY-FOUR HOUR SALAD

3 c. shredded iceberg
  lettuce or any
  combination of lettuce
2 c. grated carrots
1 stalk celery, diced
1 c. finely diced onions
1½ c. frozen green peas
Salt and pepper to taste
2 c. nonfat Mozzarella
  cheese, grated
1 (8 oz.) can sliced water
  chestnuts, drained
½ c. fat-free Parmesan
  cheese
1 pt. fat-free mayonnaise
  or salad dressing
½ c. fat-free sour cream

In a very large salad bowl, line the bottom with bite-size pieces of lettuce. Cover the lettuce with carrots, celery, onions, water chestnuts, and peas. Spread the pint of mayonnaise mixed with fat-free sour cream on top as if you are icing a cake. Sprinkle Mozzarella and Parmesan cheeses on top. Cover and refrigerate for 24 hours. Makes 16 servings.

Per serving:
Calories: 89
Fat: Less than 1 gram
Percentage of calories from fat: 1%

MEXICAN PASTA SALAD

8 oz. eggless fusilli (long
   curly pasta)
1½ c. salsa
¾ c. chopped red onion
2 tomatoes, cored and
   chopped
1 red bell pepper,
   chopped
1 green pepper, chopped
1 c. cooked black beans
   (if canned, rinsed and
   drained)
1 c. cooked fresh corn
1 c. diced jicama
½ avocado, diced
Fresh cilantro

Cook pasta according to package directions, omitting salt. Drain and cool to room temperature. Mix with about ½ of salsa and remaining ingredients. Serve garnished with fresh cilantro sprigs and red onion rings. Makes 6 servings.

Variations: Garnish with ¼ cup sunflower seeds. Add 2 grilled chicken breasts (skinless), diced.

Per serving:
Calories: 303
Fat: 4 grams
Percentage of calories from fat: 11%

NEW POTATO SALAD WITH GREEN GODDESS DRESSING

6 medium size red new
   potatoes
¼ c. reduced calorie
   mayonnaise
3 Tbsp. plain low-fat
   yogurt
1 Tbsp. plus 1 tsp.
   minced fresh parsley
1 Tbsp. lemon juice
2 tsp. minced chives
2 tsp. vinegar
½ tsp. dried whole
   tarragon
Dash of garlic powder
6 cherry tomatoes

Place potatoes in a medium saucepan; cover with water and bring to a boil. Cover; reduce heat and cook 20 minutes or until tender. Drain and slice potatoes into a serving bowl. Chill.

Combine next 8 ingredients in a small bowl. Spoon dressing over potatoes. Before serving, arrange cherry tomatoes on top of salad. Makes 6 servings.

Per serving:
Calories: 137
Fat: 2 grams
Percentage of calories from fat: 15%

ORIENTAL SALAD

¼ c. skim buttermilk
¼ c. finely chopped
  scallions
2 tsp. white wine vinegar
1 tsp. low-sodium soy
  sauce
½ tsp. granulated sugar
¼ tsp. freshly ground
  black pepper
2 c. torn Boston lettuce
  leaves
1¼ c. diced jicama
1 c. blanched trimmed
  snow peas
½ c. shredded carrots

To prepare dressing, in small bowl, combine buttermilk, scallions, vinegar, soy sauce, sugar, and pepper; set aside.

In medium salad bowl, combine lettuce, jicama, snow peas, and carrots. Add buttermilk dressing; toss to coat. Makes 4 servings.

Per serving:
Calories: 53
Fat: Less than 1 gram
Percentage of calories from fat: 6%

CREAMY POTATO SALAD

2½ c. cubed medium red
  potatoes (about 1 lb.)
½ c. nonfat buttermilk
¼ c. lemon juice
2 Tbsp. cholesterol-free
  reduced calorie
  mayonnaise or salad
  dressing
1 Tbsp. Dijon mustard
1 Tbsp. chopped fresh or
  1 tsp. dried thyme
  leaves
½ tsp. salt
½ c. chopped celery
  (about 1 medium stalk)
½ c. chopped green bell
  pepper (about 1 small)

Heat 1½ quarts water to boiling in 2 quart saucepan. Add potatoes. Cover and heat to boiling; reduce heat. Simmer 15 to 20 minutes or until tender; drain.

Mix buttermilk, lemon juice, mayonnaise, mustard, thyme, and salt in large glass or plastic bowl. Add potatoes, celery, and bell pepper; toss. Cover and refrigerate about 2 hours or until chilled. Makes 6 servings.

Per serving:
Calories: 96
Fat: 1 gram
Percentage of calories from fat: 13%

ROAST BEEF AND PASTA SALAD

1 (16 oz.) pkg. frozen
  vegetables and pasta in
  a garlic seasoned sauce
1/2 c. fat-free peppercorn
  ranch or ranch salad
  dressing
6 oz. cooked roast beef
  (from deli), cut into thin
  bite-size strips
6 cherry tomatoes
  (optional)

Cook vegetable-pasta mix according to package directions; *do not drain*. Add salad dressing and roast beef to pasta mixture; toss to coat well. Cover and chill several hours, stirring once or twice. Garnish with halved cherry tomatoes. Makes 4 servings.

Per serving:
Calories: 294
Fat: 8 grams
Percentage of calories from fat: 24%

TACO SALAD

1 head lettuce, washed
  and torn into bite-size
  pieces
1 tomato, chopped
1/2 red onion, chopped
8 oz. nonfat Cheddar
  cheese, shredded
1 can red kidney beans,
  drained
4 oz. ground turkey breast
1 pkg. taco seasoning
1 (8 oz.) pkg. corn
  tortillas, baked crisp
Nonfat sour cream
Nonfat French dressing

Cook turkey until well done; add seasoning and kidney beans until heated through. In salad bowl, combine lettuce, tomato, onion, and cheese; mix well. On individual plates, place a serving of the salad, a serving of meat /bean mixture, and a dollop of sour cream; drizzle entire plate with French dressing. Serve with chips or if you prefer, crumble chips and sprinkle in your salad. Makes 8 servings.

Per serving:
Calories: 185
Fat: 1 gram
Percentage of calories from fat: 5%

TUNA SALAD

1 (7 oz.) can light tuna in
   water (preferably low-
   sodium)
2 ribs celery, chopped
2 Tbsp. sweet pickle
   relish (or more to taste)
1 hard cooked white of
   egg, chopped
1 heaping tsp. minced
   onion
2 Tbsp. plain nonfat
   yogurt
1 Tbsp. reduced calorie
   mayonnaise
¼ tsp. dry mustard
Freshly ground black
   pepper to taste

Drain the tuna and put it in a small mixing bowl. Add the celery, relish, egg white, and onion; mix well. In another small bowl, whip together the yogurt, mayonnaise, and dry mustard. Pour over the tuna mixture and fold in gently but thoroughly. Season with the black pepper.

To make tuna sandwiches, an all-American favorite, use either sourdough bread or whole wheat, lightly toasted, or rye bread. Instead of slathering the bread with mayonnaise, use just a dab of the reduced calorie kind and add thin cucumber slices and leaves of arugula or lettuce. Makes 4 to 5 sandwiches.

Per serving:
Calories: 87
Fat: 2 grams
Percentage of calories from fat: 20%

TUNA-PASTA SALAD

1 (8 oz.) pkg. macaroni
1 (10 oz.) pkg. frozen
   peas
2 small (6½ oz.) cans
   water-packed tuna,
   drained
1 to 2 scallions, minced
2 Tbsp. mayonnaise
¾ c. plain low-fat yogurt
1 Tbsp. prepared mustard
1 tsp. garlic powder
Black pepper to taste
½ tsp. salt

Cook macaroni; drain and reserve. Cook peas and drain. In a large bowl, combine remaining ingredients. Add macaroni and peas; mix lightly. Chill. Makes 8 (1 cup) servings.

Per serving:
Calories: 213
Fat: 4 grams
Percentage of calories from fat: 16%

VEGETABLES

BAKED BEANS

1 can kidney beans (no
  salt added)
1 can lima or buttered
  beans
1 can pork and beans
1 large onion
½ c. catsup
1 tsp. mustard
½ c. brown sugar
1 Tbsp. margarine
  (unsalted)

Drain and mix all of the beans. Brown onion in margarine. Combine all remaining ingredients with beans and onion mixture. Bake for 2 hours in 300° oven, uncovered. Makes 6 servings.

Per serving:
Calories: 264
Fat: 3 grams
Percentage of calories from fat: 10%

CREOLE LIMA BEANS

1 (8 oz.) can stewed
  tomatoes
1 (10 oz.) pkg. frozen
  lima beans
1 large stalk celery,
  chopped (¾ c.)
¾ tsp. salt
⅛ tsp. pepper

Heat tomatoes to boiling. Stir in remaining ingredients. Heat to boiling again. Separate beans with a fork; reduce heat. Cover and simmer until beans are tender, about 5 minutes. Makes 4 servings.

Per serving:
Calories: 112
Fat: Less than 1 gram
Percentage of calories from fat: 1%

MEXICAN BEAN BAKE

1 c. variety baking mix
¼ c. salsa
1 (16 oz.) can refried
  beans
1 (4 oz.) can chopped
  green chilies
  (undrained)
¾ c. salsa
¾ c. shredded low-fat
  Cheddar cheese (3 oz.)
1 c. shredded lettuce
½ c. chopped tomato
  (about 1 small)
¼ c. plain nonfat yogurt

Heat oven to 375°. Spray square baking dish, 8x8x2 inches, with nonstick cooking spray. Mix baking mix, ¼ cup salsa, the beans, and chilies. Spread in dish. Top with ¾ cup salsa and the cheese. Bake, uncovered, about 30 minutes or until set. Let stand 5 minutes before cutting. Top with lettuce, tomato, and yogurt. Makes 4 servings.

Per serving:
Calories: 367
Fat: 10 grams
Percentage of calories from fat: 24%

REFRIED BEANS

1 tsp. acceptable
  vegetable oil
2 Tbsp. finely chopped
  onion
2 cloves garlic, minced
2 (15 oz.) cans no-salt-
  added pinto beans
1 Tbsp. reduced sodium
  ketchup
2 Tbsp. canned, diced
  green chili peppers

In large, nonstick skillet, heat oil over medium heat. Add onion and saute about 5 minutes, or until soft. Add garlic and saute another 2 to 3 minutes. Set aside. Drain beans well, reserving liquid. Put beans in shallow bowl and mash with a potato masher or fork. Add ½ cup of reserved bean liquid and ketchup; mash again. Add bean mixture and chili peppers to the sauteed garlic and onion. Mix well. Heat over medium heat, stirring constantly, until beans are thoroughly heated. Makes 5 servings.

Per serving:
Calories: 126
Fat: 1 gram
Percentage of calories from fat: 10%

BROCCOLI CHEESE-RICE CASSEROLE

2 boxes long grain and
  wild rice (5 minute
  variety, cooked using
  liquid butter substitute)
2 pkg. frozen chopped
  broccoli, prepared as
  directed
1 (14 oz.) can fat-free
  chicken broth (low salt
  variety)
2 (8 oz.) cans chopped
  mushrooms, rinsed and
  drained
2 (8 oz.) cans whole water
  chestnuts, rinsed and
  drained
2 c. grated nonfat
  Cheddar cheese
1 c. crushed seasoned
  stuffing cubes
1 to 1½ tsp. salt-free
  extra spicy seasoning

Prepare the rice as directed on the package. Add the cooked broccoli, mushrooms, water chestnuts, and chicken broth to the rice mixture. Add seasoning and the grated nonfat cheese. Spoon into a large casserole dish that has been sprayed with a nonfat cooking spray. Top with homemade low-fat croutons. Bake at 350°F. for 30 to 35 minutes, covered. Remove cover the last 10 minutes. Makes 16 servings.

Per serving:
Calories: 145
Fat: 1 gram
Percentage of calories from fat: 4%

GLAZED CARROTS

3 c. ¼ inch slices carrots
(about 6 medium)
½ c. water
½ c. dry white wine or
apple juice
2 tsp. margarine
1 tsp. ground ginger
1 Tbsp. lemon juice
2 tsp. packed brown
sugar

Cook all ingredients, except lemon juice and brown sugar, in 10 inch skillet over medium heat 12 to 15 minutes, stirring occasionally, until liquid has evaporated. Reduce heat to medium-low. Stir in lemon juice and brown sugar. Cook 5 minutes, stirring occasionally, until carrots are glazed. Makes 6 servings.

Per serving:
Calories: 65
Fat: 1 gram
Percentage of calories from fat: 24%

COLESLAW

3 c. thinly sliced green
cabbage
3 c. thinly sliced red
cabbage
2 carrots, shredded
1 sweet green or yellow
pepper, julienned
2 scallions, minced
⅓ c. fat-free mayonnaise
⅓ c. nonfat plain yogurt
3 Tbsp. white wine
vinegar
½ tsp. ground black
pepper
⅛ tsp. celery seeds

In a large salad bowl, toss the red and green cabbages, carrots, peppers, and scallions.

In a small bowl, whisk the mayonnaise, yogurt, vinegar, pepper, and celery seeds. Pour over the salad and toss. Chill. Makes 8 servings.

Per serving:
Calories: 42
Fat: Less than 1 gram
Percentage of calories from fat: 4%

CORN-CARROT CASSEROLE

2 c. carrots, diced and
cooked
½ c. kernel corn, drained
½ tsp. salt
4 slices nonfat American
cheese
½ c. nonfat cracker
crumbs
3 Tbsp. flour
⅔ c. skim milk
½ c. onion, chopped fine

Combine flour, milk, salt, and onion in pan sprayed with nonstick spray. Cook over medium heat until thick; add cheese. Put vegies in 8x8 inch pan sprayed with nonstick spray. Pour cheese mixture over vegies. Top with crumbs. Bake 25 minutes at 350°. Makes 10 servings.

Per serving:
Calories: 64
Fat: Less than 1 gram
Percentage of calories from fat: 3%

HONEY-GLAZED CARROTS

1½ lb. baby carrots (fresh
  or frozen)
½ c. water
1 Tbsp. acceptable
  margarine
½ Tbsp. brown sugar
2 Tbsp. honey
2 to 3 Tbsp. minced fresh
  parsley

Rinse and trim carrots, if fresh. Bring water to a boil in a medium saucepan. Add carrots; reduce heat, cover, and simmer about 10 minutes, or until carrots are tender-crisp. Drain.

If using frozen carrots, follow package directions for cooking.

In a nonstick skillet, melt margarine over medium-high heat. Add sugar, honey, and carrots. Reduce heat and turn carrots frequently until well glazed, 1 to 2 minutes. Sprinkle with parsley before serving. Makes 6 servings.

Per serving:
Calories: 86
Fat: 3 grams
Percentage of calories from fat: 25%

OVEN ROASTED POTATO WEDGES

4 baking potatoes,
  scrubbed
Vegetable cooking oil
  spray
1 Tbsp. grated Parmesan
  cheese, divided

Preheat oven to 450°. Halve potatoes lengthwise; cut halves lengthwise into long wedges. Spray potatoes with cooking spray. Place on cooking sheet, cut side down. Sprinkle with 1½ teaspoons cheese and dust with paprika; bake 15 minutes. Turn potato wedges; sprinkle with remaining cheese and dust with additional paprika. Bake 15 minutes longer or until crisp. Makes 4 servings.

Per serving:
Calories: 185
Fat: 1 gram
Percentage of calories from fat: 3%

MAC 'N CHEESE

3 Tbsp. liquid butter
    substitute
1½ to 2 Tbsp. flour
½ tsp. lite salt (optional)
½ tsp. pepper
2 c. skim milk
1 Tbsp. liquid butter
    substitute
2 c. elbow or shell
    macaroni, cooked
1 Tbsp. grated onion
    (optional)
½ tsp. lite salt (optional)
¼ to ½ tsp. pepper
2 c. grated nonfat
    Cheddar cheese
½ c. crushed seasoned
    cubed style stuffing

Prepare white sauce by combining butter substitute, flour, salt, pepper, and slowly adding skim milk. Stir with a wire whisk until smooth and thickened. Set aside. Place half of the cooked macaroni in the bottom of a 2 quart glass casserole dish that has been sprayed with a nonfat cooking spray. Sprinkle with half of the onion, salt, pepper, and cheese. Repeat. Pour sauce over the casserole. Drizzle 1 tablespoon liquid butter substitute over the top.

Sprinkle remaining cheeses over this. Sprinkle crushed stuffing cubes on top. Cover and bake for 30 minutes at 350°F. Uncover and bake 10 minutes longer. Makes 9 servings.

Per serving:
Calories: 126
Fat: Less than 1 gram
Percentage of calories from fat: 3%

SCALLOPED POTATOES

3½ lb. baking potatoes
    (about 7 large), peeled
    and sliced ⅛ inch thick
    (10 c.)
4 oz. Cheddar cheese,
    shredded (1 c.)
½ c. sliced green onions
1 tsp. salt
½ tsp. pepper
2 Tbsp. all-purpose flour
3 c. low fat milk

Preheat oven to 350°. Grease a shallow 3 quart baking dish. Layer half the potatoes over bottom of prepared dish. Sprinkle with half the cheese, green onions, salt, and pepper. Cover with remaining potatoes. Put flour into a medium bowl. Whisk in milk until blended. Pour evenly over potatoes. Sprinkle with remaining cheese, green onions, salt, and pepper. Bake, uncovered, 60 to 70 minutes, or until potatoes are very tender and top is lightly browned. Makes 12 servings.

Per serving:
Calories: 165
Fat: 4 grams
Percentage of calories from fat: 24%

MASHED POTATOES

4 large, all-purpose
   potatoes
Half an onion, peeled
   (optional)
½ tsp. butter substitute
   per potato (or more to
   taste)
½ c. evaporated skim
   milk (or more to taste)
Salt and freshly ground
   black pepper to taste
Nutmeg (optional)

Peel the potatoes; quarter them and put them in a pot with the optional onion. Cover with cold water and boil, covered, until just tender, about 20 minutes. (Check with the tip of a sharp knife.) Don't overcook, or the potatoes will be waterlogged.

Drain the potatoes in a colander. Discard onion if used. Return potatoes to pot and briefly shake dry over heat. Sprinkle with butter substitute. Cover and let sit 5 minutes. Mash the potatoes, then switch to a whisk and beat in enough milk to give a pleasing consistency. Season to taste with salt and pepper, more butter substitute (if you wish), and several gratings of nutmeg if you like. Makes 4 servings.

Per serving:
Calories: 182
Fat: Less than 1 gram
Percentage of calories from fat: 1%

STEAMED NEW POTATOES WITH GARLIC SAUCE

8 small or 4 large new
   potatoes (about 1¼ lb.,
   unpeeled), scrubbed
   and, if large, cut in
   halves
2 heads garlic
2 tsp. skim milk
1 tsp. acceptable
   vegetable oil
1 tsp. nonfat "butter"
   granules
2 tsp. chopped fresh
   parsley
Freshly ground black
   pepper to taste

In a medium saucepan, place a steamer basket and add water to a depth of 1 to 2 inches. Be sure the water does not reach the bottom of the basket. Cover saucepan and bring to a boil over medium-high heat. Place potatoes in steamer basket. Separate cloves of garlic, but do not peel the paper-thin skins surrounding each clove. Scatter cloves around potatoes. Cover and steam about 20 minutes, or until a fork can be easily inserted into potatoes.

Remove garlic from pan. Remove skins from garlic cloves by peeling them off with your hands or by pushing the garlic pulp out of the cloves. Discard skins and mash garlic pulp with milk, oil, and "butter" granules.

Remove potatoes from pan and cut them in halves. Serve with a dollop of garlic sauce, parsley, and pepper. Makes 4 servings.

Per serving:
Calories: 157
Fat: 1 gram
Percentage of calories from fat: 7%

ROSEMARY-BAKED RED POTATOES

2¼ lb. new potatoes
¼ c. finely chopped
   shallots (about 2 large)
2 Tbsp. chopped fresh or
   2 tsp. crushed dried
   rosemary leaves
2 Tbsp. olive or vegetable
   oil

Heat oven to 350°. Spray rectangular pan, 13x9x2 inches, with nonstick cooking spray. Place potatoes in pan. Sprinkle with shallots and rosemary. Drizzle with oil; stir to coat. Bake, uncovered, about 1¼ hours, stirring occasionally, until potato skins are crisp and potatoes are tender. Makes 6 servings.

Per serving:
Calories: 195
Fat: 5 grams
Percentage of calories from fat: 22%

TWICE-BAKED POTATOES

4 (8 oz.) russet potatoes,
   scrubbed
¾ c. 1% low-fat cottage
   cheese
¼ c. sliced green onions
2 Tbsp. skim milk
¼ tsp. salt
⅛ tsp. pepper
¼ c. shredded Cheddar
   cheese (1 oz.)

Preheat oven to 400°. Arrange potatoes directly on oven rack and bake 45 to 55 minutes, or until tender when pierced with a fork. When cool enough to handle, split open tops and, working over medium bowl, scoop out potatoes, leaving ¼ inch thick shells. Add remaining ingredients, except cheese, to bowl and mash until blended and smooth. Spoon mixture into shells; sprinkle tops with cheese. Arrange in a shallow baking pan. Return to oven and bake about 15 minutes, or until filling is hot and cheese is melted.

To microwave: Prick potatoes all over with a fork. Arrange in spoke pattern on a paper towel in microwave oven. Microwave on HIGH (100% power) 10 to 12 minutes, turning and rearranging potatoes once, until almost tender. Let stand 5 minutes, or until fork-tender. Split potatoes; prepare filling, and stuff shells as directed, but *do not* top with cheese. Arrange in a spoke pattern in a shallow baking dish. Microwave on HIGH 5 to 7 minutes until filling is hot. Sprinkle tops with cheese; let stand 3 minutes until cheese melts. Makes 4 servings.

Per serving:
Calories: 242
Fat: 3 grams
Percentage of calories from fat: 11%

STUFFED SWEET POTATOES

2 (6 oz.) baked sweet
  potatoes, halved
  lengthwise
½ c. drained crushed
  pineapple
¼ c. raisins
1 Tbsp. plus 1 tsp.
  reduced calorie tub
  margarine
½ tsp. pumpkin pie spice
Dash of salt

Preheat oven to 400°F. Scoop out pulp from potato halves into mixing bowl, leaving ¼ inch shells. Mash pulp; reserve shells.

Add remaining ingredients to potato pulp; stir to combine. Spoon potato mixture evenly into reserved shells; place on baking sheet and bake until heated through, about 10 minutes. Makes 4 servings.

Per serving:
Calories: 136
Fat: 2 grams
Percentage of calories from fat: 13%

VEGETABLE FRIED RICE

1 egg substitute (¼ c.)
  plus 1 egg white
1 Tbsp. liquid butter
  substitute or 1 Tbsp.
  fat-free chicken broth
2 tsp. minced garlic (in a
  jar)
½ c. thinly sliced celery
¼ c. chopped green
  pepper
½ c. sliced green onion
  (reserve tops)
¼ c. thinly sliced carrots
2 c. cooked rice
1 c. bean sprouts
4 Tbsp. low sodium soy
  sauce
1 Tbsp. lemon juice
1 Tbsp. cooking sherry
¼ tsp. ground ginger

Pour eggs into a nonstick skillet sprayed with a nonfat cooking spray. Cook until set in 1 large pancake. Remove from pan, cool, cut into thin strips, and reserve. Heat 1 tablespoon liquid butter substitute or chicken broth in pan, adding garlic, celery, green pepper, green onion (not tops), and carrot. Brown, stirring constantly, for about 2 minutes. Add cooked rice. Stir constantly until heated through and slightly browned. Stir in bean sprouts. Mix together soy sauce, lemon juice, cooking sherry, and ginger; pour over all. Place on serving dish and sprinkle on egg strips and tops of green onions. Makes 8 servings.

Per serving:
Calories: 93
Fat: Less than 1 gram
Percentage of calories from fat: 4%

TOMATO AND BROCCOLI CASSEROLE

2 c. frozen cooked
   chopped broccoli,
   drained
1½ c. cooked elbow
   macaroni (4 oz. dry)
1 medium onion, chopped
1 tsp. minced garlic (in a
   jar)
2 Tbsp. liquid butter
   substitute or 2 Tbsp.
   fat-free chicken broth
5 medium tomatoes,
   peeled, seeded, and
   chopped
1 c. snipped parsley
1 tsp. instant chicken
   broth granules
¼ tsp. lite salt (optional)
¼ tsp. crushed oregano
¼ tsp. crushed basil
1 c. grated nonfat
   Cheddar cheese

Set aside cooked and drained broccoli. In a 3 quart saucepan, cook onion and garlic in liquid butter substitute or chicken broth. Add tomatoes, parsley, bouillon granules, salt, oregano, and basil. Bring to a boil. Reduce heat and cover, simmering 3 minutes. Stir in pasta and ½ cup of the cheese. Add broccoli. Pour the broccoli mixture into an 8x8x2 inch glass casserole dish that has been sprayed with a nonfat cooking spray. Bake, uncovered, in a 375°F. oven for 15 minutes. Sprinkle remaining cheese on top and bake 5 minutes longer. Makes 10 servings.

Per serving:
Calories: 93
Fat: 1 gram
Percentage of calories from fat: 5%

MIXED VEGETABLE PASTA

2 Tbsp. fat-free chicken
  broth
6 oz. spaghetti
  (uncooked)
Nonfat cooking spray
1 c. broccoli florets
1 c. thinly sliced carrots
1 c. sliced zucchini
¼ c. sliced onion
1 small sweet yellow
  pepper, cut in julienne
  strips
1 c. sliced fresh
  mushrooms
1 small tomato, cut into 8
  wedges
2 Tbsp. white cooking
  wine
¼ c. plus 2 Tbsp. fat-free
  Parmesan cheese
1 Tbsp. minced fresh
  parsley
¼ tsp. sweet red pepper
  flakes

Cook pasta according to package directions. Drain and set aside. Coat a large nonstick skillet with a nonfat cooking spray. Place over medium heat until hot. Add the chicken broth, broccoli, and next 3 ingredients; saute 4 minutes. Add pepper strips and mushrooms; saute 4 minutes longer. Add pasta, tomato, and white cooking wine; toss gently. Cook until thoroughly heated. Sprinkle with cheese, parsley, and pepper flakes; toss gently. Serve immediately. Makes 9 servings.

Per serving:
Calories: 104
Fat: 1 gram
Percentage of calories from fat: 5%

MAIN DISHES

FAJITAS WITH PICO DE GALLO

2 Tbsp. fresh lime juice
2 tsp. vegetable oil
2 garlic cloves, crushed
1 lb. flank steak or
  boneless beef top sirloin
  steak, cut ¾ inch thick
Pico de Gallo (recipe
  follows)
1 green or red bell
  pepper, seeded and cut
  into strips
1 onion, halved and sliced
8 flour tortillas (8 inch
  size), warmed
Lime wedges (optional)
Cilantro sprigs (optional)

Pico de Gallo:
½ c. diced zucchini
½ c. seeded chopped
  tomato
¼ c. chopped cilantro
¼ c. prepared picante
  sauce or salsa
1 Tbsp. fresh lime juice

In sealable plastic bag, combine lime juice, oil, and garlic; add steak, turning to coat. Close bag securely and marinate in refrigerator 20 to 30 minutes, turning bag over once. Meanwhile, prepare Pico de Gallo.

Preheat broiler. Remove steak from marinade; discard marinade. Place steak on rack in broiler pan so surface of meat is 2 to 3 inches from heat. Broil 12 to 14 minutes for rare to medium doneness, turning once. During last 5 minutes of cooking, add pepper and onions; broil until tender-crisp, turning once.

To serve, carve steak across the grain into slices; roll up in tortillas with peppers, onions, and Pico de Gallo. Garnish with lime wedges and cilantro sprigs. Makes 4 servings.

Pico de Gallo: In medium bowl, combine all ingredients; mix well.

Per serving:
Calories: 590
Fat: 17 grams
Percentage of calories from fat: 27%

GRILLED ROUND STEAK WITH TOMATILLO SAUCE

1½ lb. beef top round
  steak (about ¾ inch
  thick)
¾ c. burgundy or other
  dry red wine
2 Tbsp. lime juice
1 Tbsp. Worcestershire
  sauce
½ tsp. seasoned salt
Dash of pepper
1 clove garlic, minced
Vegetable cooking spray

Tomatillo Sauce:
½ lb. fresh tomatillos
1 small onion, chopped
1 clove garlic, peeled
½ c. loosely packed
  cilantro leaves
1 Tbsp. vegetable oil
½ tsp. sugar
½ tsp. salt

Trim excess fat from steak. Place steak in a large shallow baking dish. Combine next 6 ingredients in a small bowl; mix well and pour over steak. Cover and refrigerate 24 hours, turning steak occasionally.

Remove steak from marinade. Coat grill with cooking spray. Grill 5 to 6 inches over hot coals 5 to 7 minutes on each side or until desired degree of doneness. Transfer steak to a cutting board; cut steak across grain into ¼ inch thick slices. Serve immediately with equal amounts of Tomatillo Sauce per serving. Makes 6 servings.

Tomatillo Sauce: Remove stems and other husks of tomatillos; rinse well. Combine all ingredients in container of an electric blender; process until smooth. Transfer tomatillo mixture to a medium saucepan and bring to a boil. Reduce heat and simmer, uncovered, 10 minutes. Serve hot. Yield: About 1 cup.

Per serving:
Calories: 211
Fat: 7 grams
Percentage of calories from fat: 30%

MARINATED COCKTAIL MEATBALLS

1¼ lb. chopped beef
½ c. bread crumbs
1 egg
¼ c. water
1 tsp. prepared mustard
1 Tbsp. parsley flakes
Pinch of oregano
1 grated onion
Garlic salt
1 tsp. dried mint
1 tsp. Worcestershire
  sauce
½ c. tomato sauce
¼ c. water

Mix all ingredients, except tomato sauce and ¼ cup water; shape into 1 inch balls. Put on lightly greased baking pan and bake in a 450° oven for 20 minutes. Drain on absorbent paper. In a saucepan, simmer tomato sauce and ¼ cup water for 5 minutes; correct seasoning. Add meatballs to sauce and allow to marinate overnight. Heat in covered casserole and serve hot. Yield: 2 to 2½ dozen. Makes 9 servings.

Per serving:
Calories: 120
Fat: 3 grams
Percentage of calories from fat: 23%

ROAST BEEF HASH

6 (4 oz.) boiled red-
    skinned potatoes,
    peeled and cut into ¼
    inch dice
¼ c. plain low-fat yogurt
1½ tsp. Worcestershire
    sauce
½ tsp. salt
⅛ tsp. pepper
½ lb. lean cooked roast
    beef
1 Tbsp. plus 1 tsp.
    vegetable oil
Chopped parsley to
    garnish (optional)

In large bowl, mash 1 cup of the potatoes with fork or potato masher. Add yogurt, Worcestershire sauce, salt, and pepper; mash until smooth. Add remaining potatoes and the roast beef; stir to combine.

In large nonstick skillet, heat oil. Add hash and press it into a large cake. With a wooden spoon handle, poke 4 steam holes near the center. Cook over medium heat, pressing cake several times with a spatula until well browned on bottom, about 15 minutes.

To turn hash, place a large plate over skillet and turn both plate and skillet over, so hash slides onto plate. Slide back into skillet. (If cake breaks, simply patch and press together.) Cook until well browned and slide hash onto serving plate. Garnish with parsley if desired. If making ahead, reheat hash in the skillet over low heat. Makes 4 servings.

Per serving:
Calories: 291
Fat: 8 grams
Percentage of calories from fat: 25%

OPEN-FACE ROAST BEEF SANDWICHES

1-2 Tbsp. prepared
    horseradish
¼ c. reduced fat
    mayonnaise
1 Tbsp. chopped mango
    chutney
2 tsp. 1% low-fat milk
4 large slices dark rye
    bread
½ cucumber, thinly sliced
½ small red onion, thinly
    sliced
¾ lb. thinly sliced deli
    roast beef
1 Tbsp. snipped chives
Radishes (optional)

In small bowl, combine horseradish, mayonnaise, chutney, and milk. Spread one side of each bread slice with 2 teaspoons sauce. Top with equal amounts of cucumber, onion, and beef. Spoon remaining sauce evenly over beef; sprinkle with chives. Garnish sandwiches with radishes. Makes 4 servings.

Per serving:
Calories: 280
Fat: 7 grams
Percentage of calories from fat: 24%

BAKED CHICKEN BREASTS

2 split chicken breasts,
   boned and skinned
¼ c. lite Dijon vinaigrette
   salad dressing
2 Tbsp. seasoned bread
   crumbs
2 Tbsp. Parmesan cheese,
   grated

Place chicken in shallow baking dish. Pour salad dressing over chicken. Bake 40 to 45 minutes in 350° oven. Remove from heat (oven). Sprinkle bread crumbs and cheese over chicken. Return to oven for 10 minutes to brown. Makes 2 servings.

Per serving:
Calories: 355
Fat: 9 grams
Percentage of calories from fat: 25%

BARBECUED CHICKEN

Precooking the chicken in the microwave allows for a dramatic reduction in grilling time.

1 (3 lb.) chicken, wings
   and backbone removed
   and the rest skinned
   and cut into serving
   pieces
1 small onion, chopped
1 garlic clove, finely
   chopped
¼ tsp. safflower oil
1 c. tomato puree
1 Tbsp. cider vinegar
2 Tbsp. chutney
4 drops of hot red pepper
   sauce
2 Tbsp. dark brown sugar
¼ tsp. dry mustard
Freshly ground black
   pepper

Light the coals in a barbecue grill about 30 minutes before grilling time.

To prepare the barbecue sauce, combine the onion, garlic, and oil in a bowl. Cover with plastic wrap and microwave on HIGH for 2 minutes. Add the tomato puree, vinegar, chutney, red pepper sauce, brown sugar, mustard, and pepper; stir well. Cover the bowl with a paper towel and microwave on MEDIUM HIGH (70% power) for 3 minutes. Stir the sauce again and microwave on MEDIUM HIGH for 3 minutes more. Remove the sauce from the oven and let it stand while you precook the chicken.

Place the chicken pieces on a microwave roasting rack with their meatier portions toward the outside of the rack. Microwave the chicken on HIGH for 6 minutes. Set aside any pieces that have turned from pink to white, then rearrange the remaining pieces with their uncooked portions toward the outside of the rack. Continue to microwave on HIGH for periods of 2 minutes, removing the pieces that turn white.

Brush the chicken with the barbecue sauce. Grill the pieces over the hot coals for approximately 10 minutes, turning them once during the cooking and basting them often. Makes 4 servings.

Per serving:
Calories: 386
Fat: 8 grams
Percentage of calories from fat: 20%

BROILED SAGE CHICKEN

2 Tbsp. chopped fresh or
   2 tsp. dried sage leaves
2 Tbsp. chopped onion
2 Tbsp. low-fat sour
   cream
2 Tbsp. lime juice
2 tsp. Dijon mustard
½ tsp. salt
¼ tsp. pepper
6 boneless, skinless
   chicken breast halves
   (about 1½ lb.)

Mix all ingredients, except chicken breast halves, in a large glass or plastic dish. Add chicken; turn to coat with marinade. Cover and refrigerate at least 3 hours.

Set oven control to broil. Spray broiler pan with nonstick cooking spray. Place chicken in pan. Broil chicken with tops 5 to 7 inches from heat 7 minutes; turn. Broil about 7 minutes longer or until juices run clear. Makes 6 servings.

Per serving:
Calories: 135
Fat: 2 grams
Percentage of calories from fat: 13%

CAJUN CHICKEN WITH BEANS AND RICE

1 tsp. vegetable oil
3 (4 oz.) pkg. Cajun-
   flavored skinless
   boneless chicken
   breasts
½ green bell pepper,
   seeded and chopped
1 (16 oz.) can red kidney
   beans, drained
1 (14.5 oz.) can reduced
   sodium stewed
   tomatoes
1 (8 oz.) can reduced
   sodium tomato sauce
¼ tsp. dried thyme leaves
2 c. hot cooked rice

Cut chicken into ½ inch cubes. In large, nonstick saucepan over medium-high heat, heat oil. Add chicken and bell pepper; stir-fry 5 minutes. Stir in beans, stewed tomatoes, tomato sauce, and thyme; bring to a boil. Reduce heat to medium; cook 10 minutes, or until thickened, stirring occasionally. Serve over hot cooked rice. Makes 4 servings.

Per serving:
Calories: 362
Fat: 5 grams
Percentage of calories from fat: 12%

CHILI CHICKEN

6 (8 inch) flour tortillas
1 Tbsp. vegetable oil
3 Tbsp. all-purpose flour
1 lb. skinless boneless
  chicken breasts (about
  6)
1 (10 oz.) can enchilada
  sauce
1 (11 oz.) can corn
  kernels
1 (4 oz.) can whole green
  chilies
¾ c. shredded Cheddar
  cheese
Sliced green onions
  (optional)

Preheat oven to 375°. Wrap tortillas in foil and place in oven to heat while making filling.

In large nonstick skillet, heat oil. Put flour and chicken in a large plastic bag and shake to lightly coat chicken. Add chicken to skillet and cook, in batches if necessary, 1 to 2 minutes per side, or until golden. Remove to paper towels to drain. Wipe out skillet. Add enchilada sauce and corn and bring to a boil.

Meanwhile, drain and coarsely chop chilies. Arrange chicken on sauce. Top with chilies and cheese. Cover, reduce heat, and simmer 1 to 2 minutes, or until cheese melts.

Remove tortillas from oven. To serve, put 1 piece of chicken and about ⅓ cup sauce on each tortilla. Garnish with green onions. Fold or roll up to enclose filling. Makes 6 servings.

Per serving:
Calories: 406
Fat: 13 grams
Percentage of calories from fat: 29%

CHICKEN-BASIL NOODLES

2 tsp. olive or vegetable
  oil
½ c. finely chopped onion
  (about 1 medium)
1 clove garlic, finely
  chopped
2½ c. chopped tomatoes
  (about 3 medium)
2 c. cubed cooked
  chicken or turkey
¼ c. chopped fresh basil
½ tsp. salt
⅛ tsp. red pepper sauce
2 c. hot cooked
  cholesterol-free noodles

Heat oil in 10 inch nonstick skillet over medium-high heat. Saute onion and garlic in oil. Stir in remaining ingredients, except noodles; reduce heat to medium. Cover and cook about 5 minutes, stirring frequently, until mixture is hot and tomatoes are soft. Serve over noodles.

Microwave directions: Omit olive or vegetable oil. Mix all ingredients, except noodles, in ungreased 2 quart microwavable casserole. Cover loosely and microwave on HIGH 6 to 8 minutes, stirring every 2 minutes, until mixture is hot and tomatoes are soft. Serve over noodles. Makes 4 servings (¾ cup chicken mixture and ½ cup noodles each).

Per serving:
Calories: 234
Fat: 7 grams
Percentage of calories from fat: 25%

CHICKEN CHILI ENCHILADAS

1 can chicken chili
1 c. white meat chicken,
   chopped or shredded
1 c. chopped onions
½ c. salsa
1 can reduced fat cream
   of mushroom soup
1 can reduced fat cream
   of chicken soup
1 pkg. medium size flour
   tortillas
1 (8 oz.) container *fat free*
   sour cream*
½ c. taco sauce (green)
1½ c. grated nonfat
   Cheddar cheese

Mix together soups and spread ½ the mixture in a 9x13 inch pan that has been sprayed with nonstick spray. In separate bowl, combine chili, chicken, onions, and salsa. Spread about 2 tablespoons of the mixture in each tortilla and roll up; place each rolled tortilla side by side in pan on top of soup mixture. You'll have enough mixture for 10 to 12 tortillas. Spread remaining soup mixture over tortillas.

Combine sour cream (or cream cheese) and taco sauce; spread evenly over soup. Top with grated cheese. Cover with foil; bake for 35 minutes at 350°. Remove foil during the last 5 minutes of baking. Makes 12 servings.

You may garnish with chopped tomatoes, also.

* Substitute 8 ounces nonfat cream cheese if sour cream is not available.

Per serving:
Calories: 255
Fat: 5 grams
Percentage of calories from fat: 17%

CHICKEN DIVAN

4 chicken breasts, boiled
   and cut into small
   pieces
2 (10 oz.) pkg. frozen
   broccoli spears
1 can reduced fat cream
   of mushroom soup
1 can reduced fat cream
   of chicken soup
¾ c. skim milk
½ c. nonfat mayonnaise
2 Tbsp. lemon juice
½ tsp. curry powder
1 c. nonfat Cheddar
   cheese
1 c. bread crumbs

Cook broccoli; drain well and place on bottom of 9x13 inch pan. Spread chicken over broccoli. Combine soups, milk, mayonnaise, lemon juice, and curry powder; pour over chicken. Sprinkle with bread crumbs. Bake, uncovered, for 45 minutes at 350°. Makes 6 servings.

Per serving:
Calories: 296
Fat: 5 grams
Percentage of calories from fat: 14%

CHICKEN FETTUCCINE

1 lb. boned, skinned
　breasts, cut into bite-
　size pieces
½ c. chopped onion
¼ tsp. dried basil
¼ tsp. garlic powder
Pinch of lite salt
　(optional)
Pepper to taste
1 tsp. minced garlic (in a
　jar)
2 c. sliced zucchini
4 c. hot cooked fettuccine
¾ c. skimmed evaporated
　milk (1 small can)
3 Tbsp. fat-free chicken
　broth
1 (8 oz.) can stems and
　pieces mushrooms,
　rinsed and drained
¼ c. fat-free Parmesan
　cheese

Spray a large nonstick frying pan with nonfat cooking spray. Saute the onion and garlic in chicken broth. Add the basil and other seasonings. Add chicken and saute about 7 minutes or until the chicken is cooked. Add the zucchini and mushrooms. Saute until tender. Add the fettuccine and milk. Sprinkle the cheese on top and mix well. Makes 8 servings.

Per serving:
Calories: 201
Fat: 1 gram
Percentage of calories from fat: 6%

CHICKEN GYROS

3 chicken breasts, boned
　and skinned
½ c. lemon juice
2 Tbsp. mustard
2 Tbsp. minced garlic
1½ tsp. dried oregano
1 tsp. thyme
1 (8 oz.) ctn. plain nonfat
　yogurt
1 small cucumber, peeled
　and chopped
1 tsp. dill weed
¼ tsp. salt
4 pocket bread (do not
　slice)
1 tomato, sliced thin
Red onion slices

Cut chicken into thin, bite-size pieces. Place in a plastic sealable bag. Add lemon juice, mustard, garlic, oregano, and thyme. Marinate in fridge at least 6 hours (the longer you marinate, the better the flavor). Combine yogurt, cucumber, dill weed, and salt in small bowl; mix well. Cover and refrigerate at least 6 hours.

To serve: Spray skillet with nonstick spray. Drain chicken and place in skillet. Cook over medium-high heat until done. Keep chicken warm while preparing bread. Place 1 pocket bread in plastic bag and microwave on HIGH for 20 seconds. Place pocket bread on serving plate; spoon chicken down middle of bread. Top with yogurt sauce, sliced tomatoes, and onion. Fold in half and eat like a taco. Serves 4.

Per serving:
Calories: 312
Fat: 2 grams
Percentage of calories from fat: 7%

CHICKEN SPAGHETTI

1 c. chopped onion (about
  1 large)
1 c. water
1 Tbsp. chopped fresh or
  1 tsp. dried oregano
  leaves
2 tsp. chopped fresh or ¾
  tsp. dried basil leaves
1½ tsp. chopped fresh or
  ½ tsp. dried marjoram
  leaves
1 tsp. sugar
¾ tsp. chopped fresh or
  ¼ tsp. dried rosemary
  leaves
1 clove garlic, crushed
1 bay leaf
1 (8 oz.) can tomato
  sauce
1 (6 oz.) can tomato paste
1½ c. cut-up cooked
  chicken
4 c. hot cooked spaghetti

Heat all ingredients, except chicken and spaghetti, to boiling in 10 inch skillet; reduce heat. Cover and simmer 30 minutes, stirring occasionally. Stir in chicken. Cover and simmer 30 minutes longer, stirring occasionally. Remove bay leaf. Serve sauce over spaghetti. Makes 6 servings.

Per serving:
Calories: 236
Fat: 3 grams
Percentage of calories from fat: 12%

GINGER CHICKEN STIR-FRY

Vegetable cooking spray
2 (4 oz.) pkg. teriyaki-
  flavored skinless
  boneless chicken
  breasts, thinly sliced
1 Tbsp. olive oil
2 Tbsp. grated peeled
  ginger root
2 garlic cloves, minced
2 c. broccoli florets
2 to 3 carrots, cut into
  thin 2 inch strips
1 red bell pepper, seeded
  and cut into ½ inch
  pieces
1 c. snow peas
2 Tbsp. honey
2 Tbsp. dry sherry
2 Tbsp. soy sauce
2 c. hot cooked rice

Spray large skillet or wok with cooking spray. Place over medium-high heat until hot. Add chicken; stir-fry 3 to 4 minutes, or until no longer pink. Remove chicken and set aside. In same pan, heat oil. Add ginger root and garlic; stir-fry 1 minute. Add broccoli, carrots, red bell pepper, and snow peas; stir-fry 2 minutes longer, or until tender-crisp.

In small bowl, combine 3 tablespoons water, honey, sherry, and soy sauce; add to skillet. Cook 2 minutes, stirring often. Add chicken; heat thoroughly. Serve over rice. Makes 4 servings (with ½ cup rice).

Per serving:
Calories: 324
Fat: 6 grams
Percentage of calories from fat: 17%

LEMONY CHICKEN

4 skinless, boneless
   chicken breasts
½ c. fresh lemon juice
2 Tbsp. white wine
   vinegar
½ c. sliced fresh lemon
   peel
6 to 8 green onions,
   thinly sliced
1 Tbsp. chopped fresh
   oregano (or 1 tsp.
   dried)
¼ tsp. light salt
½ tsp. paprika
½ tsp. lemon pepper

Place chicken in a 9x13 inch glass baking dish. Combine lemon juice, vinegar, lemon peel, green onions, and oregano. Pour over chicken; turn to coat with marinade. Cover and refrigerate several hours or overnight. Turn occasionally.

Sprinkle chicken with salt, paprika, and lemon pepper. Cover and bake at 325° for 15 minutes. Uncover and bake an additional 10 to 15 minutes or until done. Makes 4 servings.

Per serving:
Calories: 258
Fat: 3 grams
Percentage of calories from fat: 11%

MEXICAN SPAGHETTI

1 large onion, chopped
2 garlic cloves or 1 tsp.
   minced garlic (in a jar)
¼ c. fat-free chicken
   broth
12 oz. spaghetti, broken
   into pieces
1 (24 oz.) can whole
   tomatoes (undrained)
1 (14 oz.) can fat-free
   chicken broth
2 c. cooked white meat
   chicken or white meat
   skinless turkey, cut in
   cubes
1½ c. picante sauce
1 tsp. ground cumin
1 c. grated nonfat
   Cheddar cheese

In a large skillet over medium heat, saute onion and minced garlic in chicken broth. Cook about 5 minutes. Add 14 ounces chicken broth and whole tomatoes with juice. Add spaghetti, broken into pieces, to the tomato mixture. Break up the tomatoes with a spoon. Add picante sauce and cumin, simmering covered, until spaghetti is cooked and most of the liquid is absorbed. Add chicken and spoon into casserole dish sprayed with nonfat cooking spray. Sprinkle cheese on top. Bake, covered, at 350°F. for 15 to 20 minutes until cheese is melted. Makes 8 servings.

Per serving:
Calories: 274
Fat: 2 grams
Percentage of calories from fat: 7%

DIJON CHICKEN BREASTS

The use of nonfat dry milk with a small amount of water gives a thick, creamy coating that will stick without the need of eggs.

⅓ c. Dijon mustard
¼ c. nonfat dry milk
2 Tbsp. water
¾ c. fine fresh bread crumbs (from firm-textured white bread (2 slices) or French bread)
½ tsp. chopped fresh tarragon
6 small boneless chicken breast halves, skinned
Imported Hungarian paprika
¼ c. finely chopped parsley (preferably Italian)

Preheat the oven to 350°F. Arrange the oven rack in its highest position. In a small bowl, combine the mustard, dry milk, and water; mix well. Stir in the bread crumbs and tarragon. With a rubber spatula, spread the mixture over the top of the chicken breasts which you've arranged in a nonstick baking pan. Sprinkle lightly with paprika, then the parsley. Bake, uncovered, in the upper third of the preheated oven for 20 to 25 minutes.

If you wish the tops a little browner, run the chicken breasts under the broiler for about 40 seconds, watching constantly, until some brown flecks appear. Makes 6 servings.

Per serving:
Calories: 204
Fat: 3 grams
Percentage of calories from fat: 13%

ORIENTAL BARBECUED CHICKEN

4 boneless skinless chicken breast halves (about 1 lb.)
½ c. hoisin sauce
1 Tbsp. sesame oil
1 Tbsp. no-salt-added tomato paste
½ tsp. ground ginger
2 cloves garlic, crushed

Set oven control to broil. Trim fat from chicken breast halves. Place chicken on rack in broiler pan. Mix remaining ingredients; brush on chicken. Broil with tops about 4 inches from heat 7 to 8 minutes or until brown; turn. Brush with sauce. Broil 4 to 5 minutes longer or until juices of chicken run clear. Heat remaining sauce to boiling. Serve with chicken. Makes 4 servings.

Per serving:
Calories: 200
Fat: 5 grams
Percentage of calories from fat: 23%

SPICY CHICKEN

1 c. (8 oz.) plain low-fat
  yogurt
3 Tbsp. freshly squeezed
  lemon juice
1 Tbsp. grated peeled
  fresh ginger root
1 Tbsp. paprika
1½ tsp. finely minced
  garlic
1¼ tsp. ground coriander
1¼ tsp. ground cumin
¾ tsp. ground red pepper
3 whole (1 lb. each)
  chicken breasts, split
  and skin removed

In 1 gallon size food storage bag or large bowl, mix yogurt, lemon juice, ginger root, paprika, garlic, coriander, cumin, and ground red pepper.

With small sharp knife, cut ½ inch deep slits in chicken about 1 inch apart. Put chicken in bag with yogurt mixture. Close bag and shake to coat chicken, rubbing marinade into the slits. Refrigerate at least 6 hours, but preferably overnight.

Preheat broiler; line broiler pan with foil (for easy clean-up). Lightly oil broiler pan rack.

Arrange chicken on rack bone-side up. Broil 10 minutes 4 to 6 inches from heat, then turn pieces over and broil 10 to 15 minutes longer, or until juices run clear when meat is pierced. Makes 6 servings.

Per serving:
Calories: 220
Fat: 3 grams
Percentage of calories from fat: 13%

SKILLET CHICKEN

4 split chicken breasts or
  8 thighs
2 large onions, sliced
4 Tbsp. mustard (plain
  yellow)
Pam
Pepper

Remove skin from chicken; lightly spray a frying pan with Pam. Quickly brown chicken (medium flame); reduce heat. Add onions. Add mustard; season with pepper. Place lid on frying pan. Cook till chicken is done and onions are tender, approximately 30 to 45 minutes. Makes 4 servings.

Per serving:
Calories: 169
Fat: 2 grams
Percentage of calories from fat: 12%

SPANISH CHICKEN WITH RICE

2 c. chicken broth,
  divided
1½ c. quick-cooking
  white rice
1 Tbsp. olive oil
1 lb. skinless boneless
  chicken breast halves,
  cut crosswise into strips
¼ tsp. salt
¼ tsp. pepper
¼ tsp. paprika
1 small green bell pepper,
  cut into strips
½ c. frozen chopped
  onion
½ tsp. minced garlic
1 (4 oz.) jar sliced
  pimientos, drained
1 (4½ oz.) jar sliced
  mushrooms, drained

In medium saucepan, bring 1½ cups broth to boil. Stir in rice; cover, remove from heat, and let stand while preparing chicken

In large skillet, heat oil over medium-high heat. Add chicken; sprinkle with salt, pepper, and paprika. Add bell pepper, onion, and garlic; stir-fry 3 to 4 minutes, or until chicken is golden brown. Stir in pimientos, mushrooms, and remaining ½ cup broth.

Bring to a boil, reduce heat, and simmer, uncovered, until chicken is cooked through, about 2 minutes. Serve over hot cooked rice. Makes 4 servings.

Per serving:
Calories: 327
Fat: 6 grams
Percentage of calories from fat: 16%

STUFFED CHICKEN BREAST

1 (5 oz.) chicken breast,
  skinned
⅓ c. diced onion
¼ c. diced celery
⅛ c. (2 Tbsp.) crushed
  corn flakes
1 egg
2 Tbsp. chicken stock
Salt and pepper to taste

Mix all of the ingredients together, except chicken breast. Place chicken breast on a cutting board, covered with wax paper, and pound flat. Place stuffing on one side of the chicken breast and roll up. Use toothpicks or string to hold breast together. Cover stuffed breast with a slice of lemon and bake at 350° for 15 to 20 minutes. Makes 1 serving.

Per serving:
Calories: 311
Fat: 7 grams
Percentage of calories from fat: 21%

HOT HAM SANDWICHES

½ c. butter substitute
  (reconstituted)
¼ c. mustard
¼ c. chopped onions
4 tsp. poppy seeds
8 oz. Canadian bacon or
  deli ham
8 oz. nonfat Mozzarella
  cheese
8 sandwich or dinner rolls

Combine butter substitute, mustard, onions, and poppy seeds. Spread on both halves of roll; place 1 ounce of meat on bread. Top with cheese. Wrap each roll in foil and bake 20 minutes at 350°. Makes 8 servings.

Per serving:
Calories: 253
Fat: 5 grams
Percentage of calories from fat: 20%

HAWAIIAN PIZZA

2 tsp. corn meal
1 loaf frozen white bread
   dough, thawed
1/3 c. pizza sauce
3 slices Canadian bacon,
   quartered
1 (8 oz.) can crushed
   pineapple, well drained
2 Tbsp. coarsely chopped
   green bell pepper
2 oz. (1/2 c.) shredded
   Swiss cheese

Heat oven to 450°F. Spray cookie sheets with nonstick cooking spray; sprinkle evenly with corn meal. Divide dough into thirds. Press or roll each into 7 inch circle. Place on coated cookie sheets. Prick crusts generously with fork. Bake at 450°F. for 8 minutes. (If crusts puff during baking, flatten slightly with spoon.)

Spread pizza sauce evenly over partially baked crusts. Top with remaining ingredients. Bake at 450°F. for an additional 7 to 9 minutes or until cheese is melted and crusts are golden brown. Makes 3 pizzas.

Per serving:
Calories: 565
Fat: 13 grams
Percentage of calories from fat: 21%

PORK AND BARLEY SKILLET SUPPER

2 tsp. oil
3/4 lb. boneless lean pork,
   cut into 1/2 inch cubes
1 medium onion, cut into
   thin wedges
1 c. uncooked quick-
   cooking barley
2 c. water
2 Tbsp. lite soy sauce
1/8 tsp. garlic powder
1/8 to 1/4 tsp. pepper
1 (9 oz.) pkg. frozen
   French cut green beans,
   rinsed to remove ice
   crystals and drained

Heat oil in large skillet over medium-high heat until hot. Add pork and onion. Cook and stir until pork is no longer pink. Stir in remaining ingredients, except beans. Bring to a boil. Reduce heat; cover and simmer 12 to 15 minutes or until barley is tender. Stir in beans. Bring to a boil. Reduce heat; cover and simmer an additional 5 minutes or until beans are of desired doneness. If desired, serve with additional lite soy sauce. Makes 4 servings.

Per serving:
Calories: 336
Fat: 6 grams
Percentage of calories from fat: 16%

COD FILLETS WITH VEGETABLES

4 slices bacon
8 small red potatoes
  (about 1 lb.)
½ c. sliced green onions
4 (1 inch thick) cod fillets
  (5 oz. each)
1 (14½ oz.) can sliced
  Italian style stewed
  tomatoes, drained

In large deep nonstick skillet, fry bacon until crisp. Drain well on paper towel, then crumble. Set aside. Preheat broiler. Discard all but 1 tablespoon drippings from skillet.

Cut potatoes in ⅛ inch thick slices and add to skillet; cover and cook 15 minutes over medium-low heat, stirring 2 or 3 times, until potatoes are firm-tender.

Gently stir in green onions and remove from heat. Place cod fillets over potato mixture, topping them with tomato slices. If skillet handle is plastic or wood, wrap in foil to prevent scorching. Broil 4 to 6 inches from heat about 10 minutes, or until fish is cooked through at its thickest part. Sprinkle with bacon. Serve immediately. Makes 4 servings.

Per serving:
Calories: 278
Fat: 5 grams
Percentage of calories from fat: 15%

MEXICAN BAKED FISH

1 Tbsp. canola oil
¼ c. chopped onion
2 garlic cloves, minced
1 (16 oz.) can tomatoes,
  drained and chopped
1 Tbsp. green chilies,
  chopped
1 tsp. chili powder
⅛ tsp. pepper
1 egg white
1 Tbsp. skim milk
½ c. corn meal
4 flounder fillets (1 lb.)
2 oz. part-skim
  Mozzarella cheese,
  shredded (½ c.)

Preheat oven to 325°F. In small pan over medium-high heat, saute onion and garlic in nonstick cooking spray about 3 minutes. Add tomatoes, chilies, chili powder, and pepper; bring to a boil. Reduce heat; cover and simmer 15 minutes, stirring occasionally.

In shallow dish, beat egg white and milk slightly. Place corn meal on wax paper; dip fillets in egg mixture, then in corn meal. Place fillets in baking dish sprayed with Pam (single layer). Pour sauce over fish; sprinkle with cheese. Bake about 20 minutes or until fish flakes. Makes 4 servings.

Per serving:
Calories: 266
Fat: 8 grams
Percentage of calories from fat: 26%

SEAFOOD-STUFFED PEPPERS

4½ c. water
1½ lb. fresh medium
    shrimp
8 medium size green
    peppers
Vegetable cooking spray
1 tsp. margarine
1 stalk celery, chopped
4 green onions, chopped
1 clove garlic, minced
¾ lb. lump crabmeat
1 c. cooked parboiled
    rice, cooked without
    salt or fat
1 slice whole wheat
    bread, torn into small
    pieces
½ c. (2 oz.) shredded
    Mozzarella cheese
¼ c. grated Parmesan
    cheese
2 Tbsp. chopped fresh
    parsley
⅛ tsp. pepper
Dash of hot sauce

Bring 4½ cups water to a boil; add shrimp and reduce heat. Cook 3 minutes. Drain well and rinse with cold water. Peel and devein shrimp; chop coarsely and set aside.

Cut a slice from the top of each pepper; remove seeds. Place peppers in boiling water; boil 5 minutes. Drain and set aside.

Coat a large skillet with cooking spray; add margarine and place over medium heat until margarine melts. Add celery, onion, and garlic; saute 5 minutes or until tender. Remove from heat. Add chopped shrimp and remaining ingredients; stir well.

Spoon ¾ cup seafood mixture into each pepper; arrange peppers, cut side up, in a 12x8x2 inch baking dish. Bake at 350° for 30 minutes or until thoroughly heated. Makes 8 servings.

Per serving:
Calories: 251
Fat: 5 grams
Percentage of calories from fat: 18%

TUNA NOODLE CASSEROLE

8 oz. noodles (½ lb. box)
1 Tbsp. margarine
2 Tbsp. flour
2 c. skim milk
1 (6½ oz.) can tuna
    (water packed), drained
½ c. chopped mushrooms
4 Tbsp. grated Parmesan
    cheese
¼ c. chopped onion
1 c. frozen peas, thawed
¼ tsp. thyme
¼ tsp. celery seed
¼ tsp. salt

Topping:
1 Tbsp. fine bread crumbs
1 tsp. margarine

Cook noodles in boiling water (without added salt) until al dente; drain. Melt margarine in saucepan over moderate heat and blend in flour. Slowly add milk and stir until slightly thickened. Remove from heat. Combine noodles with sauce, then mix in drained tuna and remaining ingredients, except topping. Spoon into 2 quart casserole (sprayed with vegetable oil cooking spray) and sprinkle bread crumbs over surface. Dot with margarine. Bake at 350°, covered, for 20 to 25 minutes. Makes 4 servings.

Per serving:
Calories: 404
Fat: 7 grams
Percentage of calories from fat: 15%

TUNA PITA

1 (6½ oz.) can water-
   packed low-sodium
   tuna
2 celery stalks, chopped
2 green onions, thinly
   sliced
1 Tbsp. minced fresh dill
   (or ¼ tsp. dried)
½ c. plain nonfat yogurt
2 tsp. coarse grained
   mustard
¼ tsp. celery salt
4 whole wheat pita breads
Romaine lettuce
Sliced tomato

Drain and flake tuna. Combine with celery, green onion, and dill. Blend together yogurt, mustard, and celery salt, then mix with tuna. Cut pita bread in halves and line with lettuce and tomato slices. Add tuna and serve. Makes 4 servings.

Per serving:
Calories: 239
Fat: 2 grams
Percentage of calories from fat: 8%

EASY SAUSAGE BALLS

1 lb. ground turkey breast
3 c. reduced fat biscuit
   mix
8 oz. nonfat Cheddar
   cheese
3 Tbsp. sage
3 Tbsp. seasoning salt

Mix all ingredients together and form into balls. Spray cookie sheet with nonstick spray and bake for 12 to 15 minutes at 375°. Serve with your favorite sweet and sour sauce and gourmet mustard. Makes at least 60 sausage balls. Makes 12 servings (5 sausage balls each).

Per serving:
Calories: 184
Fat: 2 grams
Percentage of calories from fat: 11%

REUBEN SANDWICHES

1 oz. turkey pastrami
¼ c. sauerkraut, drained
⅛ c. nonfat Mozzarella
   cheese
2 Tbsp. nonfat Thousand
   Island dressing
1 Tbsp. mustard
2 slices dill rye bread

Spread Thousand Island dressing on slice of bread; top with turkey pastrami, sauerkraut, and cheese. Spread mustard on second slice of bread and place on top of sandwich innards.

Using a nonstick frying pan, grill sandwich over medium heat until bread is toasted. Serve immediately with additional mustard and/or Thousand Island dressing for dipping. (If sandwich does not get hot enough to melt cheese, cover with a paper towel and place in microwave on HIGH for 1 minute.) Makes 1 serving.

Per serving:
Calories: 278
Fat: 4 grams
Percentage of calories from fat: 14%

MEXICAN LASAGNA

1 lb. ground turkey
1½ tsp. ground cumin
1 Tbsp. chili powder
¼ tsp. garlic powder
¼ tsp. red pepper
1 tsp. salt
1 tsp. black pepper
1 (16 oz.) can tomatoes,
   chopped
12 corn tortillas
2 c. small curd, nonfat
   cottage cheese, drained
1 c. nonfat shredded
   Cheddar cheese
¼ c. nonfat egg substitute
½ c. nonfat shredded
   Cheddar cheese
2 c. shredded lettuce
½ c. chopped tomatoes
3 green onions, chopped

Brown turkey; rinse in colander under hot water and drain. Add cumin, chili powder, garlic powder, red pepper, salt, pepper, and tomatoes; heat through. Spray 9x13 inch pan with nonstick spray. Cover bottom and sides of pan with ½ the tortillas. Pour beef mixture over tortillas; place another layer of tortillas over meat mixture and set aside. Combine cottage cheese, 1 cup Cheddar cheese, and egg; pour over tortillas. Bake at 350° for 30 minutes. Remove from oven; sprinkle rows of Cheddar cheese, lettuce, tomatoes, and green onions diagonally across center of casserole. Makes 8 servings.

Per serving:
Calories: 292
Fat: 8 grams
Percentage of calories from fat: 23%

TURKEY MEATBALL STROGANOFF

2 Tbsp. liquid butter
   substitute or fat-free
   chicken broth
1 lb. ground lean white
   meat skinless turkey
1/2 c. crushed cubed style
   stuffing
1/2 tsp. garlic powder
1/2 c. chopped onions
2 (8 oz.) cans rinsed and
   drained stems and
   pieces mushrooms
2 to 3 Tbsp. flour
1 tsp. minced garlic (in a
   jar)
3 env. instant chicken
   broth and seasoning
   mix
1 1/2 c. water
1 c. fat-free sour cream
4 c. hot cooked linguine
2 Tbsp. ketchup

Combine turkey, crushed seasoned cubes, and garlic powder. Form into balls. Spray large skillet with nonfat cooking spray. Brown turkey balls on all sides. Remove and drain on paper towels to remove the fat. In the same skillet, cook the onions until tender in 2 tablespoons liquid butter substitute or chicken broth. There might be enough moisture left in the pan from the turkey. Add minced garlic, mushrooms, and flour. Stir in the broth mix, ketchup, and water. Boil. Return the turkey balls to the skillet and heat but do not boil. Simmer, uncovered, about 15 to 20 minutes. Stir in sour cream, but do not boil. Serve turkey balls and sauce over cooked linguine. Makes 8 servings.

Per serving:
Calories: 238
Fat: 1 gram
Percentage of calories from fat: 4%

TURKEY POCKETS

2 onions
1 green bell pepper
1 Tbsp. olive oil
1 lb. ground, skinless
   white meat turkey
1 1/2 tsp. ground cumin
1 tsp. minced garlic
3/4 c. water
1/4 c. tomato paste
1/3 c. golden raisins
1/4 c. small pimiento-
   stuffed green olives
1/4 tsp. pepper
4 (6 inch) pitas

Halve onions lengthwise, then cut crosswise in thin strips. Finely chop bell pepper. In large skillet, heat oil over high heat. Add turkey and cumin; cook, stirring often to break up pieces, 5 minutes, or until meat is no longer pink. Transfer turkey to a bowl with a slotted spoon. Add onions to skillet. Cook 4 minutes, stirring often, until onions are tender. Add bell pepper and garlic. Cook 3 minutes, stirring constantly, until tender-crisp.

Return turkey to skillet. Add water, tomato paste, raisins, olives, and pepper. Stir until boiling. Reduce heat and simmer, uncovered, 8 minutes, or until slightly thickened.

Cut pitas in halves. Spoon 1/2 cup turkey mixture into each half. Makes 4 servings.

Per serving:
Calories: 408
Fat: 7 grams
Percentage of calories from fat: 15%

BROCCOLI LASAGNA

2 (10¾ oz.) cream of
broccoli soup
1 (10 oz.) pkg. frozen
chopped broccoli
3 carrots, sliced thin
1 large onion, diced
¾ lb. mushrooms, sliced
12 lasagna noodles
2 (8 oz.) pkg. reduced fat
Mozzarella cheese
1 (15 oz.) container no fat
Ricotta cheese
4 egg whites

About 2½ hours before serving, heat undiluted broccoli soup and frozen broccoli until broccoli is thawed in 2 quart saucepan over medium low heat. Spray 10 inch skillet with nonstick cooking spray.

Over medium high heat, cook carrots and onion until lightly browned. Reduce heat to low; stir in ¼ cup water. Cover; simmer 15 minutes, or until tender. Remove to a bowl. In same skillet (resprayed), cook mushrooms until lightly browned and all liquid is gone. Stir in carrot mixture while vegetables are cooking. Prepare noodles. Drain.

In bowl, mix Mozzarella, Ricotta, and eggs. Preheat oven to 375°. In 9x13 inch dish, spread 1 cup broccoli sauce. Arrange ½ of noodles over sauce. Top with ½ of cheese mixture, then all the carrot mixture and ½ of remaining sauce. Top with remaining noodles, cheese mixture, and sauce. Bake 45 minutes. Let stand 10 minutes before serving. Makes 8 servings.

Per serving:
Calories: 430
Fat: 13 grams
Percentage of calories from fat: 28%

CHILES RELLENOS CASSEROLE

Nonstick spray coating
2 (4 oz.) cans chopped
green chilies, drained
6 oz. reduced fat Cheddar
cheese, shredded
2 c. skim milk
1 c. packaged low fat
biscuit mix
1 c. refrigerated or frozen
egg product, thawed
1 c. low-fat cottage
cheese
Salsa (optional)

Spray 2 quart rectangular baking dish with nonstick spray. Sprinkle with chilies and Cheddar cheese. Combine milk, biscuit mix, and egg product in a medium bowl; use a wire whisk or fork to beat till smooth. Stir in cottage cheese. Spoon mixture over chilies and cheese. Bake, uncovered, in a 350° oven about 45 minutes or till puffed and a knife inserted near the center comes out clean. Let stand 10 minutes before serving. Top with salsa if desired. Makes 8 servings.

Per serving:
Calories: 183
Fat: 6 grams
Percentage of calories from fat: 29%

FETTUCCINE WITH TOMATO SAUCE

¼ c. finely chopped onion (about 1 small)
2 cloves garlic, crushed
⅔ c. low-fat Ricotta cheese
1 Tbsp. chopped fresh or 1 tsp. dried basil leaves
1 Tbsp. chopped fresh chives
2 tsp. sugar
⅛ tsp. pepper
1 (14.5 oz.) can whole tomatoes (undrained)
1 (16 oz.) pkg. fettuccine

Spray 2 quart saucepan with nonstick cooking spray; heat until hot. Cook and stir onion and garlic in saucepan over medium heat until onion is tender. Stir in remaining ingredients, except fettuccine; break up tomatoes with a spoon. Heat to boiling; reduce heat. Simmer, uncovered, about 5 minutes, stirring occasionally, until mixture thickens slightly.

Meanwhile, cook fettuccine as directed on package; drain. Rinse with hot water; drain. Place fettuccine back in pan; toss with tomato sauce. Sprinkle with additional chives if desired. Makes 5 servings.

Per serving:
Calories: 419
Fat: 4 grams
Percentage of calories from fat: 9%

FETTUCINI WITH FRESH HERBS

Grow basil and parsley on your window sill for this simple dish.

4 oz. eggless fettucini
1 clove garlic, minced
1 Tbsp. olive oil
¼ c. chopped fresh parsley
⅓ c. chopped fresh basil
2 tomatoes, cored and chopped
Freshly ground black pepper

Cook pasta according to package directions, omitting salt. Drain. Saute garlic in olive oil until golden. Add pasta, herbs, and chopped tomato. Season to taste with black pepper. Makes 4 servings.

Per serving:
Calories: 153
Fat: 4 grams
Percentage of calories from fat: 24%

ITALIAN CASSEROLE

8 oz. uncooked wheel-
    shaped macaroni
    (about 3½ c.)
8 oz. bulk turkey Italian
    sausage
1 (4 oz.) can mushroom
    stems and pieces,
    drained
¼ c. sliced ripe olives
2¾ c. meatless spaghetti
    sauce
1 c. shredded fat-free or
    part-skim Mozzarella
    cheese (4 oz.)

Heat oven to 350°. Cook macaroni as directed on package; drain. Cook sausage in skillet, stirring frequently, until no longer pink; drain. Mix macaroni, sausage, and remaining ingredients, except cheese, in ungreased 2½ quart casserole.

Cover and bake about 30 minutes or until hot. Sprinkle with cheese. Let stand 5 minutes or until cheese is melted. Makes 6 servings.

Per serving:
Calories: 302
Fat: 5 grams
Percentage of calories from fat: 16%

MACARONI AND CHEESE

1 (7 oz.) pkg. macaroni
    and cheese (with
    powdered cheese-sauce
    packet)
2 Tbsp. skim milk
⅓ c. low-fat sour cream

Cook the noodles according to package directions, omitting salt. Drain, then add milk and sour cream instead of the butter or margarine called for on the package. Mix well to coat evenly. Add contents of the cheese-sauce packet; mix well. Serve hot. Makes 3 servings.

Per serving:
Calories: 277
Fat: 4 grams
Percentage of calories from fat: 14%

PASTA WITH GARLIC AND HERBS

1 lb. rotini or other spiral-shaped pasta
1 c. plain low-fat yogurt
2 Tbsp. chopped parsley
1 Tbsp. chopped fresh oregano
2 Tbsp. chopped fresh thyme
1 Tbsp. chopped fresh mint
2 Tbsp. virgin olive oil
½ garlic clove, finely chopped
¼ tsp. salt
Freshly ground black pepper

Bring 4 quarts of lightly salted water to a boil in a large pot and cook the pasta until it is *al dente*, approximately 9 minutes.

While the pasta is cooking, combine the yogurt, parsley, oregano, thyme, mint, oil, and garlic in a small bowl; season the mixture with the salt and some freshly ground black pepper.

When the rotini is cooked, drain it in a colander, but leave a little of the cooking water clinging to the pasta. This will thin the herb, yogurt, and garlic mixture to form a sauce. Stir the herb mixture into the hot pasta and serve it immediately. Makes 8 servings.

Per serving:
Calories: 259
Fat: 5 grams
Percentage of calories from fat: 16%

PITA TACOS

2 tsp. vegetable oil
½ c. chopped onion
½ c. chopped green bell pepper
6 oz. drained cooked red kidney beans
1 c. tomato sauce
2 tsp. red wine vinegar
1 tsp. honey
¼ tsp. Mexican seasoning
4 small (1 oz.) pita breads, cut to form pockets
½ c. shredded lettuce
½ c. chopped tomato
1½ oz. shredded Cheddar cheese

In medium nonstick skillet, heat oil; stir in onion and pepper. Cook over medium heat until onion is translucent, about 2 minutes. Stir in beans, tomato sauce, vinegar, honey, and seasoning. Reduce heat; simmer, stirring occasionally, 10 minutes. Cool slightly.

Spoon equal amount of bean mixture into each pita; top evenly with lettuce, tomato, and cheese. Makes 4 servings.

Per serving:
Calories: 219
Fat: 7 grams
Percentage of calories from fat: 26%

SOUTHWEST SCRAMBLED EGGS

2 tsp. vegetable oil
3 corn tortillas (about 6
   inches in diameter), cut
   into thin strips
¼ c. chopped onion
   (about 1 small)
2 c. egg substitute
   fat/cholesterol-free
   product
½ jalapeno chili, seeded
   and chopped
1 c. salsa
¼ c. low-fat sour cream
2 Tbsp. chopped green
   onions (with tops)

Heat oil in 10 inch nonstick skillet over medium-high heat. Cook tortillas and ¼ cup onion in oil about 5 minutes, stirring frequently, until tortillas are crisp.

Mix egg substitute and chili. Pour over tortilla mixture; reduce heat to medium. As mixture begins to set at bottom and side, gently lift cooked portions with spatula so that thin, uncooked portion can flow to bottom. Do not stir. Cook 4 to 5 minutes or until eggs are thickened throughout but still moist. Top each serving with salsa, sour cream, and green onions. Makes 4 servings.

Per serving:
Calories: 175
Fat: 4 grams
Percentage of calories from fat: 20%

VEGETARIAN HOT DISH

1 c. uncooked regular rice
1 medium onion, chopped
   (½ c.)
2 garlic cloves, minced
2 Tbsp. oil
1 medium zucchini,
   coarsely chopped (1 c.)
1 medium green pepper,
   chopped (1 c.)
½ tsp. oregano leaves
¼ tsp. salt
⅛ tsp. pepper
2 medium tomatoes,
   peeled and coarsely
   chopped (2 c.)
16 oz. can (2 c.) kidney
   beans, drained
2 oz. (½ c.) shredded
   Cheddar cheese

Cook rice as directed on package, omitting or reducing salt to ½ teaspoon. In large skillet, saute onion and garlic in oil until onion is tender. Add zucchini, green pepper, oregano, salt, and pepper; cook vegetables until crisp-tender, about 5 minutes. Add tomatoes and beans; cover and heat thoroughly. Spoon hot rice onto serving platter. Spoon vegetable mixture over rice; sprinkle with cheese. Makes 7 servings.

Per serving:
Calories: 230
Fat: 7 grams
Percentage of calories from fat: 28%

BREADS, ROLLS

APPLE-RAISIN SPICE BREAD

3 small apples (unpeeled), shredded
½ c. plus 2 Tbsp. raisins
¾ c. boiling water
1½ c. whole wheat flour
½ tsp. baking powder
1 tsp. baking soda
1 tsp. ground cinnamon
½ tsp. ground allspice
⅛ tsp. ground cloves
1 Tbsp. plus 1 tsp. vegetable oil
¼ c. skim milk
2 egg whites
1 tsp. vanilla extract
¼ c. packed brown sugar

In a small bowl, combine apples and raisins. Add boiling water. Cover and let stand until cool. Preheat oven to 350°. Lightly oil a 4x8 inch loaf pan or spray with a cooking spray. In a large bowl, combine flour, baking powder, baking soda, and spices; mix well.

In another bowl, combine remaining ingredients. Beat with a fork or wire whisk until blended. Add to dry ingredients along with apple mixture. Mix until all ingredients are moistened. Place mixture in prepared pan. Bake 45 minutes until a toothpick inserted in the center comes out clean. Cool in pan on wire rack 5 minutes, then turn onto rack to finish cooling. Makes 8 servings.

Per serving:
Calories: 191
Fat: 3 grams
Percentage of calories from fat: 13%

BANANA SPICE BREAD

1¾ c. all-purpose flour (or bread flour)
2 tsp. baking powder
½ tsp. ground cinnamon
¼ tsp. ground cloves
¼ tsp. lite salt (optional)
¼ c. oat bran
2 egg substitutes (½ c.)
1 c. packed brown sugar
⅓ c. liquid butter substitute
3 medium size ripe bananas, mashed (1½ c.)

Preheat oven to 350°F. Spray a 9x5 inch loaf pan with a nonfat cooking spray. Sift flour, baking powder, cinnamon, cloves, and lite salt into a medium size bowl. Stir in oat bran; set aside. In another medium size bowl, beat together egg substitute, brown sugar, and liquid butter substitute; add bananas. Add dry ingredients to banana mixture. Beat until just combined. Pour into prepared loaf pan. Bake in oven for 50 minutes. Remove from pan. Cool on wire rack. Makes 16 servings.

Per serving:
Calories: 135
Fat: 1 gram
Percentage of calories from fat: 4%

ORANGE CHOCOLATE CHIP BREAD

1 c. skim milk
¼ c. orange juice
⅓ c. sugar
1 egg, slightly beaten
1 Tbsp. freshly grated
   orange peel
3 c. all-purpose biscuit
   baking mix
½ c. semi-sweet
   chocolate chips

Heat oven to 350°F. Grease 9x5x3 inch loaf pan. In medium bowl, combine milk, orange juice, sugar, egg, and orange peel; stir in baking mix. Beat with spoon until well combined, about 1 minute. Stir in mini chips. Pour batter into prepared pan. Bake about 45 to 50 minutes or until wooden pick inserted in center comes out clean. Cool 10 minutes; remove from pan to wire rack. Cool completely. Slice and serve. To store leftovers, wrap in foil or plastic wrap. Makes 16 servings.

Per serving:
Calories: 146
Fat: 5 grams
Percentage of calories from fat: 30%

CORN BREAD

¼ c. canola oil
1½ c. yellow corn meal
   (whole grain if possible)
1½ c. whole wheat flour
⅓ c. instant powdered
   nonfat milk
½ tsp. salt
1½ Tbsp. baking powder
3 Tbsp. sugar (optional)
3 large egg whites
1½ c. skim milk

Preheat oven to 450°F. Pour 1 tablespoon of oil into a 10½ inch cast iron skillet or into a 9x11 inch ovenproof glass casserole dish. Set aside.

In a bowl, mix corn meal, flour, powdered milk, salt, baking powder, and sugar. Set aside. In another bowl, beat egg whites with a whisk until slightly frothy. Add milk and remaining oil; whisk again.

Pour liquid ingredients into dry ingredients and mix, but do not overmix (some lumps will remain). Place skillet or dish in oven 3 or 4 minutes to heat the oil. *Be careful not to let it burn!* Watch the time carefully.

Pour batter into hot skillet or dish. Bake 20 minutes. Immediately remove from pan by turning onto a cutting board. Cut into 12 wedges or squares. Serve immediately. Makes 12 servings.

Per serving:
Calories: 196
Fat: 5 grams
Percentage of calories from fat: 24%

STRAWBERRY BREAD

3 c. all-purpose flour
½ tsp. lite salt (optional)
4 egg substitute (1 ctn., 1 c.)
1½ c. liquid butter substitute
2 c. sugar
1 tsp. baking soda
1 tsp. cinnamon
2 (10 oz.) pkg. frozen strawberries, thawed
1 c. whole grain wheat and barley cereal

Cream together egg substitute, liquid butter substitute, sugar, and strawberries. Sift together the dry ingredients and blend with strawberry mixture. Stir in cereal. Pour into 3 loaf pans (8 ½ x 4½ inches) that have been sprayed with a nonfat cooking spray. Bake at 350°F. for 55 to 60 minutes. Cool on a wire rack. Makes 36 servings.

Per serving:
Calories: 113
Fat: Less than 1 gram
Percentage of calories from fat: 3%

FRUITY MUFFINS

1¼ c. fat-free plain yogurt or plain low-fat yogurt
½ c. packed brown sugar
¼ c. vegetable oil
2 egg whites
1¼ c. whole wheat flour
¾ c. oat bran
¼ c. corn meal
1 tsp. baking powder
½ tsp. baking soda
¼ tsp. salt
½ c. chopped dried fruit (apricots, peaches, apples, or figs)
½ c. cooked whole-grain triticale or brown rice

Heat oven to 400°. Spray 12 medium muffin cups, 2½ x 1¼ inches, with nonstick cooking spray, or line with paper baking cups. Beat yogurt, brown sugar, oil, and egg whites in large bowl. Stir in remaining ingredients, except dried fruit and triticale, just until flour is moistened. Fold in dried fruit and triticale. Divide batter evenly among muffin cups (cups will be very full). Sprinkle with brown sugar if desired. Bake 20 to 22 minutes or until golden brown. Immediately remove from pan. Makes 12 servings.

Per serving:
Calories: 177
Fat: 5 grams
Percentage of calories from fat: 26%

OAT AND RAISIN BRAN MUFFINS

1¼ c. oat bran
1¼ c. bran cereal with
   raisins
2 c. whole wheat flour
½ c. brown sugar
1 tsp. cinnamon
1 c. raisins
2 to 3 tsp. baking powder
2 c. skim milk
½ c. egg substitute
½ c. molasses
¼ c. fat-free margarine

Combine dry ingredients in a large bowl. In a different bowl, blend milk, molasses, egg substitute, and margarine. Add liquid ingredients with dry ingredients until moistened. Spray nonfat cooking spray on muffin papers in pan. Fill each cup ¾ full. Bake at 425°F. for 15 minutes.

Options: Add 4 mashed bananas to the muffin mixture. Add 2 tablespoons grated orange peel and 3 tablespoons orange juice. Add 2 cups chopped apricots to the mixture. Add 2 cups diced green apples to mixture before baking. Makes 36 servings.

Per serving:
Calories: 80
Fat: 1 gram
Percentage of calories from fat: 6%

PUMPKIN MUFFINS

1 c. raisins
½ c. water
½ c. egg substitute
1 c. pumpkin
1 c. sugar
¾ tsp. cloves
¾ tsp. cinnamon
¼ tsp. salt
⅓ c. oil
1¾ c. flour
1½ tsp. baking powder
½ tsp. baking soda

Soak raisins in ½ cup water for 5 minutes. Beat egg substitute; stir flour, baking powder, and baking soda together. Add pumpkin mixture with ½ raisin mixture; mix well. Add remaining raisins; stir. Fill muffin pans ⅔ full. Bake at 400° for 25 to 30 minutes. Makes 12 servings.

Per serving:
Calories: 248
Fat: 7 grams
Percentage of calories from fat: 24%

CORN BREAD DRESSING

¼ c. water
1½ c. chopped celery
1 c. chopped onion (about
    1 medium)
3 c. corn bread crumbs
4 slices stale or toasted
    whole-grain bread, cut
    into cubes
1 tsp. rubbed sage
¼ c. chopped fresh
    parsley
1 tsp. poultry seasoning
1½ c. chicken stock
2 large egg whites, lightly
    beaten
Vegetable oil spray
1 Tbsp. margarine

Preheat oven to 350°F. In a small saucepan, boil the water. Add celery and onion; cook 2 to 3 minutes, or until soft. In a medium bowl, toss corn bread crumbs, bread cubes, sage, parsley, and poultry seasoning to mix well. Add chicken stock and egg whites; mix again. Pour the celery, onions, and cooking liquid into the bowl; mix well.

Spray a 2 quart casserole with vegetable oil spray. Pour mixture into prepared casserole and dot with margarine. Bake, uncovered, 30 minutes. Serve immediately. Makes 7 servings.

Per serving:
Calories: 263
Fat: 5 grams
Percentage of calories from fat: 15%

CORN PANCAKES

¾ c. flour
1 tsp. salt
Dash of cayenne
1⅓ c. cream style corn
1 Tbsp. baking powder
Black pepper to taste
1 egg, lightly beaten

Mix flour, baking powder, salt, pepper, and cayenne. Blend in egg. Add corn and mix well. Using a tablespoon, drop mixture into a hot Pam sprayed skillet or onto a griddle, a few at a time. Cook until golden; turn with spatula and cook the second side. Makes 4 servings, 3 (3 inch) pancakes.

Per serving:
Calories: 167
Fat: 2 grams
Percentage of calories from fat: 10%

FRENCH TOAST

1 thick slice sourdough
    bread
Egg substitute to equal 1
    egg
2 Tbsp. skim milk
Dash of vanilla

Mix egg substitute, milk, and vanilla in bowl. Dip the bread in the bowl to soak up the mixture. Spray griddle with Pam. Makes 1 serving.

Per serving:
Calories: 141
Fat: 3 grams
Percentage of calories from fat: 20%

GERMAN APPLE PANCAKE

Pam
1 large egg
6 Tbsp. flour
6 Tbsp. skim milk
½ apple, sliced
2 Tbsp. brown sugar
Cinnamon to taste
1 egg white

Preheat oven to 425°F. Place rack in upper third of oven. Spray 10 inch pie plate with Pam and put in oven. Beat egg and white slightly, then add and stir in flour and milk. Batter will be lumpy.

Toss apple with sugar and cinnamon. Arrange on top of batter in hot pie plate. Bake 15 minutes at 425°. Makes 2 servings.

Per serving:
Calories: 219
Fat: 3 grams
Percentage of calories from fat: 12%

PANCAKES

1 large egg
1 egg white
1¼ c. skim milk
Dash of vanilla
Dash of salt
1 c. flour
1 tsp. baking powder
Dash of nutmeg

Beat egg and white lightly in bowl; add milk, vanilla, salt, nutmeg, flour, and baking powder. Beat briefly. Let batter set a few minutes before using. Pour ¼ cup portions of batter on griddle sprayed lightly with Pam. Makes 4 servings (3 pancakes each).

Per serving:
Calories: 163
Fat: 2 grams
Percentage of calories from fat: 9%

DESSERTS

FRUIT-TOPPED ANGEL FOOD CAKE

Angel food cake, made without fat or even yolks, is the perfect answer to a sweet tooth. It's delicious without any topping at all, and you can leave out the almond flavoring if you like.

¾ c. powdered sugar
½ c. cake flour
¾ c. egg whites (about 6)
¾ tsp. cream of tartar
½ c. granulated sugar
½ tsp. vanilla
¼ tsp. almond extract
⅛ tsp. salt
Fruit Topping (recipe
    follows)
2 Tbsp. flaked coconut,
    toasted

Fruit Topping:
½ (2.8 oz.) pkg. whipped
    topping mix (1 env.)
3 Tbsp. powdered sugar
½ c. skim milk
¼ tsp. coconut extract
1 c. cut-up pared mango
    (about 1 medium)
½ c. cut-up pared kiwi
    fruit (about 1 medium)

Heat oven to 350°. Mix powdered sugar and flour; reserve. Beat egg whites and cream of tartar in large bowl on high speed until foamy. Beat in granulated sugar, 2 tablespoons at a time, on high speed, adding vanilla, almond extract, and salt with last addition of sugar. Continue beating until stiff and glossy. Do not underbeat.

Sprinkle sugar-flour mixture, ¼ cup at a time, over meringue, folding in just until mixture disappears. Spread batter in ungreased loaf pan, 9x5x3 inches. Bake 25 to 35 minutes or until cracks feel dry and top springs back when touched lightly. Snap spring-type wooden clothespins on corners of pan for "legs." Invert pan about 2 hours or until cake is completely cool. (Or, invert pan, resting edges of pan on 2 other inverted pans to cool.) Remove from pan. Top each serving with Fruit Topping. Sprinkle with coconut.

Fruit Topping: Mix topping mix (dry), powdered sugar, milk, and coconut extract in small deep bowl. Beat on high speed 2 to 3 minutes or until thick and fluffy. Fold in mango and kiwi fruit. Makes 8 servings (with ⅓ cup topping each).

Per serving:
Calories: 206
Fat: 3 grams
Percentage of calories from fat: 11%

BLUEBERRY COFFEE CAKE

Batter:
1¼ c. all-purpose flour
2 tsp. baking powder
½ c. skim milk
2 egg whites, well beaten
½ c. sugar
½ tsp. cinnamon
3 Tbsp. oil
½ tsp. vanilla

Topping:
1½ c. fresh or frozen
  blueberries
½ tsp. cinnamon
2 Tbsp. sugar
2 Tbsp. chopped pecans

Preheat oven to 350°F. Oil 8x8 inch pan lightly. For batter, combine flour, sugar, baking powder, and cinnamon in medium bowl. Make a well in center. Combine milk, oil, eggs, and vanilla. Add all at once to flour mixture. Stir until dry ingredients are moistened and liquid is evenly distributed. Pour batter into pan.

For topping, spread blueberries over top of batter. Combine sugar and cinnamon. Spoon over blueberries. Sprinkle with nuts. Bake at 350° for 40 minutes, or until wooden pick inserted in center comes out clean. Makes 9 servings.

Per serving:
Calories: 199
Fat: 6 grams
Percentage of calories from fat: 27%

BLUEBERRY UPSIDE-DOWN CAKE

Nonstick cooking spray
¼ c. packed brown sugar
4 Tbsp. light corn syrup
1 Tbsp. lemon juice
1 c. fresh or frozen
  blueberries
1 c. all-purpose flour
⅔ c. granulated sugar
⅓ c. cornstarch
2 tsp. baking powder
½ tsp. salt (optional)
2 egg whites
⅔ c. skim milk
1 tsp. vanilla extract

Heat oven to 350°F. Spray 9 inch layer cake pan with cooking spray. Add brown sugar, corn syrup, and lemon juice; stir to combine. Place cake pan in oven 3 minutes; remove. Add blueberries to pan in even layer; set aside. In large bowl, combine flour, sugar, 2 tablespoons cornstarch, baking powder, and salt (if desired). In medium size bowl, using fork or whisk, mix egg whites, milk, remaining corn syrup, and vanilla. Add to flour mixture; stir until smooth. Carefully spoon batter over blueberries, smoothing top. Bake until toothpick inserted in center comes out clean, about 35 to 40 minutes (do not overbake). Remove pan from oven; immediately run narrow spatula or table knife around edge of pan. Invert cake onto serving plate. Serve warm or cooled. Delicious served with low calorie whipped topping. Makes 12 servings.

Per serving:
Calories: 153
Fat: Less than 1 gram
Percentage of calories from fat: 1%

CARROT CAKE WITH VANILLA SAUCE

Cake:
1½ c. liquid butter
    substitute (or 1½ c. fat-
    free margarine)
1 c. sugar
1 c. brown sugar
4 egg substitute (1 c.)
3 c. self-rising flour
2 tsp. cinnamon
½ tsp. nutmeg
¼ tsp. ground cloves
1 (8 oz.) can crushed
    pineapple (undrained)
2 tsp. vanilla
3 c. grated carrots
1 c. raisins
1 c. whole grain, wheat,
    and barley cereal

Sauce:
1 c. butter substitute
⅔ c. sugar
2 to 3 Tbsp. cornstarch
1 Tbsp. vanilla

Cream together butter substitute, sugars, egg substitute, pineapple, and vanilla. Add raisins and cereal. Add flour and spices. Fold in grated carrots. Pour into Bundt pan sprayed with nonfat cooking spray. Bake at 350°F. for 45 minutes to 1 hour.

While the cake is baking, combine all the sauce ingredients in a saucepan and cook on the stove. Bring to a boil, stirring occasionally. Bring to a full boil and stir for 1 minute. Remove from heat. After cake is baked, cool upright in pan for 5 minutes. Remove from pan. Pour ⅓ of the sauce over the cake and save the rest to be served with the cake. If sauce is lumpy, use a hand mixer and beat until smooth. If the sauce is too thin, add a little more cornstarch. Makes 16 servings.

Per serving:
Calories: 322
Fat: 1 gram
Percentage of calories from fat: 2%

CHOCOLATE CAKE

No stick cooking spray
1¼ c. flour
1 c. sugar
½ c. unsweetened cocoa
¼ c. corn starch
½ tsp. baking soda
½ tsp. salt
4 egg whites
1 c. water
½ c. light/dark corn
    syrup

Preheat oven to 350°F. Spray 9 inch square baking pan with cooking spray. In large bowl, combine dry ingredients until well mixed. In medium bowl, whisk egg whites, water, and corn syrup. Stir into dry ingredients until smooth. Pour into prepared pan. Bake 30 minutes or until cake springs back when lightly touched. Cool on wire rack 10 minutes. Makes 16 servings.

Per serving:
Calories: 137
Fat: Less than 1 gram
Percentage of calories from fat: 3%

HOT FUDGE PUDDING CAKE

1 c. self-rising flour
½ c. sugar
2 Tbsp. cocoa
½ c. skim milk
2 Tbsp. liquid butter
  substitute
1 c. whole grain, wheat,
  and barley cereal
1 c. brown sugar, packed
¼ c. cocoa
1¾ c. hot water

Heat oven to 350°F. Measure flour, granulated sugar, and 2 tablespoons cocoa into a bowl. Blend in milk and butter substitute. Stir in cereal. Pour into a square pan sprayed with a nonfat cooking spray. Stir together brown sugar and ¼ cup cocoa; sprinkle over batter. Pour hot water over batter. Bake 45 minutes. While hot, cut into squares; invert onto a dessert plate and spoon sauce over each serving. If desired, top with Dream Whip. This is a sure-to-please-everyone-dessert. Cake and sauce bake in the same pan. Makes 16 servings.

Per serving:
Calories: 142
Fat: Less than 1 gram
Percentage of calories from fat: 2%

7 MINUTE FAT-FREE FROSTING

1 c. sugar
⅓ c. water
¼ tsp. cream of tartar
Dash of lite salt
2 unbeaten egg whites
1 tsp. vanilla

Combine sugar, water, cream of tartar, and salt in a saucepan. Bring to boiling, stirring until sugar dissolves. Very slowly add sugar syrup and vanilla to the egg whites in a bowl. Beat constantly with a hand mixer until stiff peaks form, about 7 minutes. This recipe will frost the top and sides of two 8 or 9 inch layers or one 10 inch tube cake (2 cups). One serving equals 1 tablespoon.

Per serving:
Calories: 29
Fat: 0 grams
Percentage of calories from fat: 0%

FRESH LEMON COOKIES

1 c. all-purpose flour
2 tsp. baking powder
⅛ tsp. salt
2 Tbsp. margarine,
   softened
½ c. sugar
1 egg
1 Tbsp. grated lemon rind
2 Tbsp. lemon juice
Vegetable cooking spray

Combine flour, baking powder, and salt in a small bowl; set aside. Cream margarine in a medium bowl until light and fluffy. Gradually add sugar, beating well. Add egg, lemon rind, and lemon juice; beat well. Add flour mixture and stir until blended.

Drop dough by heaping teaspoonfuls onto cookie sheets lightly coated with cooking spray. Bake at 350° for 10 minutes or until edges are lightly browned. Cool slightly on cookie sheets; remove to wire racks and cool completely. Makes 28 servings.

Per serving:
Calories: 42
Fat: 1 gram
Percentage of calories from fat: 21%

BASIC GRAHAM CRACKER CRUST

1½ c. crushed cinnamon
   graham crackers (fat-
   free - about 1 pkg.)
2 Tbsp. sugar
1½ Tbsp. liquid butter
   substitute

Crush the graham crackers by placing pieces on wax paper and rolling over them with a rolling pin. Add all of the ingredients and mix with a fork until moistened. Press into a pie pan that has been sprayed with a nonfat cooking spray. Makes 8 servings (one 9 inch crust).

Per serving:
Calories: 79
Fat: 0 grams
Percentage of calories from fat: 0%

PASTRY PIE CRUST

1 c. all-purpose flour
¾ tsp. lite salt (optional)
4 Tbsp. fat-free margarine
2 to 3 Tbsp. cold water

Preheat oven to 475°F. Mix together all of the ingredients. Stir with a fork until thoroughly mixed. Do not overwork the dough. Shape this mixture into a ball and place it between 2 pieces of wax paper that have been dusted with flour. Roll the pastry into a circle large enough to fit in a 9 inch pie pan. Spray pan with a nonfat cooking spray. Arrange crust in pan. Cut off the edges that hang over. Prick the bottom with a fork. Bake 10 minutes or until golden brown. Cool before adding filling. If you are making a pie where the filling needs to be cooked with the shell, simply bake at 350°F. for 45 minutes or however long the recipe calls for. Work foil over edges while baking so the crust won't get overbrown. Remove foil for the last 5 minutes. Makes 8 servings (1 pie crust).

Per serving:
Calories: 59
Fat: Less than 1 gram
Percentage of calories from fat: 2%

APPLE CRISP

1 (21 oz.) can apple pie
    filling
¾ c. sugar
¾ c. brown sugar
½ c. flour
½ c. quick oats
1 tsp. cinnamon
½ tsp. nutmeg
1 env. dry butter
    substitute (not diluted)
2 tsp. water

Heat oven to 375°F. Mix together apple filling, water, and granulated sugar in a bowl. In another bowl, mix together all the dry ingredients. Fold the 2 together and spoon into a square baking dish that has been sprayed with a nonfat cooking spray. Bake about 30 to 40 minutes until set and golden brown on top. This is great served warm with nonfat frozen yogurt. Makes 9 servings.

As a variation, you can substitute cherry pie filling, blueberry, strawberry, or raspberry.

Per serving:
Calories: 257
Fat: 1 gram
Percentage of calories from fat: 2%

BAKLAVA

1 c. raisins
1/3 c. finely chopped
   pecans or walnuts
8 sheets phyllo dough
1/4 c. nonfat margarine (1/2
   stick), melted
1/2 c. honey
2 tsp. ground cinnamon

Preheat oven to 350°F. In a small bowl, mix raisins and nuts. Set aside.

Lightly brush each other sheet of phyllo with melted margarine and stack the sheets on top of each other. Spread raisin-nut mixture over the phyllo, leaving a 1 inch border on all sides. Drizzle honey over the top and sprinkle with cinnamon.

Roll lengthwise, jelly-roll fashion, and place on a nonstick baking sheet, making sure that the ends of the roll are tucked under and the seam side faces down. Brush the top lightly with remaining margarine. Cut through the pastry to the raisin-nut mixture, at 1½ inch intervals, to provide vents for steam to escape. Bake 20 to 30 minutes, or until light golden brown. Slice, using vent lines as guides. Makes 12 servings.

This recipe freezes well. Prepare as above but omit the final brushing with margarine and the baking. Freeze overnight on a baking sheet, then wrap well in freezer paper or foil. To prevent the pastry from getting soggy, do not defrost before baking. Place on a baking sheet, brush with margarine, and bake 35 to 45 minutes, or until golden.

Per serving:
Calories: 216
Fat: 4 grams
Percentage of calories from fat: 18%

FROZEN BANANA DESSERT CUPS

2 extra-ripe, medium
   bananas, peeled
1 c. fresh or frozen
   strawberries
1 (8 oz.) can crushed
   pineapple in juice,
   drained
2 Tbsp. honey
Dash of ground nutmeg
1 c. frozen whipped
   topping, thawed
1/4 c. chopped almonds
1 c. light cherry juice
1 Tbsp. cornstarch
1 Tbsp. sugar
Sliced fresh fruit (for
   garnish)

Place bananas, strawberries, pineapple, honey, and nutmeg in blender. Process until smooth. Fold in whipped topping and almonds.

Line 12 muffin cups with foil liners. Fill with banana mixture. Cover and freeze until firm. Blend cherry juice, cornstarch, and sugar in small saucepan. Cook, stirring, until sauce boils and thickens. Cool.

To serve, spoon cherry sauce onto each serving plate. Remove foil liners from dessert. Invert on top of sauce. Arrange fresh fruit around mold. Makes 12 servings.

Per serving:
Calories: 88
Fat: 3 grams
Percentage of calories from fat: 27%

BANANA SPLIT DESSERT

½ gal. vanilla nonfat
   frozen yogurt, softened
   slightly
4 bananas, split
   lengthwise
2 Tbsp. chocolate syrup
2 Tbsp. caramel syrup
1 (10 oz.) low-fat pound
   cake, sliced
Strawberries
Nonfat whipped topping
   (spray can)

In a 9x13 inch pan, spread ½ the frozen yogurt. Put cake slices on top of this; drizzle lightly with chocolate and caramel syrups. Cover with remaining frozen yogurt; freeze until firm.

When ready to serve, slice into 18 pieces. Serve with strawberries and banana slices. Garnish with nonfat whipped topping. Makes 18 servings.

Per serving:
Calories: 157
Fat: Less than 1 gram
Percentage of calories from fat: 7%

BLUEBERRY-PEACH CRUMBLE

6 ripe peaches
1 Tbsp. fresh lemon juice
¼ c. sugar
3 c. fresh blueberries,
   picked over and
   stemmed, or 3 c. frozen
   whole blueberries

Crumble topping:
¾ c. whole wheat flour
1 tsp. baking powder
¼ tsp. salt
1 Tbsp. cold unsalted
   butter
½ c. plus 1 Tbsp. sugar
1 egg
½ tsp. ground cinnamon
1 Tbsp. wheat germ

Preheat the oven to 375°F. Blanch the peaches in boiling water until their skins loosen, 30 seconds to 1 minute. Peel the peaches and halve them lengthwise, discarding the pits. Cut each peach half into 5 or 6 slices. In a bowl, gently toss the slices with the lemon juice and the sugar.

To prepare the crumble topping, put the flour, baking powder, salt, butter, and ½ cup of the sugar into a food processor; mix the ingredients just long enough to produce a fine-meal texture. Alternatively, put the dry ingredients into a bowl and cut the butter in using a pastry blender or 2 knives. Add the egg and blend it in, 5 to 10 seconds. The topping should have the texture of large crumbs.

Arrange the peach slices in an even layer in a large, shallow baking dish. Scatter the blueberries over the peach slices, then sprinkle the topping over the blueberries. Stir together the cinnamon, wheat germ, and the remaining tablespoon of sugar; strew this mixture over the topping. Bake the dish until the topping is brown and the juices bubble up around the edges, 45 to 55 minutes. Makes 8 servings.

Per serving:
Calories: 212
Fat: 3 grams
Percentage of calories from fat: 11%

FRESH BLUEBERRY PIE

For this pie, a tender biscuit crust encases a luscious fruity filling. The biscuit crust is easy to handle and roll and it contributes much less fat than a traditional pastry one.

2⅓ c. unbleached flour
3 tsp. baking powder
⅓ c. canola oil
½ c. skim milk
1 c. sugar
½ tsp. cinnamon
4 c. fresh blueberries

Coat a 9 inch pie plate with nonstick spray. Set aside.

In a medium bowl, whisk 2 cups of the flour with the baking powder. Add the oil and milk; mix the dough until it forms a ball. Divide the dough in half. Between waxed paper, roll out one of the halves until it fits into the pie plate. Remove the top sheet of paper and invert the dough into the plate. Remove the remaining sheet of waxed paper.

In a large bowl, gently mix the remaining ⅓ cup of flour, the sugar, cinnamon, and blueberries. Fill the pie shell with the blueberry filling.

Trim any dough that extends beyond the edge of the plate. Add the trimmed pieces to the remaining dough half and roll it out between waxed paper. Invert over the pie. Seal and flute the edges of the crust; make slits in the middle.

To prevent excessive browning, cover the edge of the crust with a 1½ inch wide strip of foil. Bake at 425°. After 20 minutes, remove the foil; continue baking until the crust is nicely browned and juice begins to bubble through the slits, 15 to 20 minutes. Serve slightly warm. Makes 1 pie (8 servings).

Per serving:
Calories: 372
Fat: 10 grams
Percentage of calories from fat: 24%

BREAD PUDDING

6 thin slices bread
   (toasted or stale), cut in
   cubes
3 c. milk (skim or 1%)
8 oz. ctn. egg substitute
¼ tsp. salt
1 tsp. vanilla
½ c. raisins (optional)

Beat together milk, egg substitute, salt, sugar, and vanilla. Add bread and raisins. Put in lightly greased baking dish. Stand dish in pan of hot water 1 inch deep. Bake at 350° for 45 minutes to 1 hour till knife inserted in middle comes out clean. Makes 10 servings.

Per serving:
Calories: 112
Fat: 2 grams
Percentage of calories from fat: 13%

BROWNIES

3 oz. unsweetened
   chocolate, chopped
1 c. granulated sugar
¾ c. flour
¾ c. 2% low-fat cottage
   cheese
3 egg whites
1 tsp. vanilla extract
¼ tsp. salt
Powdered sugar

Heat oven to 350°F. Over very low heat, melt chocolate and cool slightly. In food processor, puree all ingredients, except chocolate and powdered sugar, until smooth. Add melted chocolate. Blend well. Pour into lightly buttered, 8 inch square pan. Bake 20 to 25 minutes or until just set. Sprinkle with powdered sugar. Cut into squares. Makes 16 servings.

Per serving:
Calories: 117
Fat: 3 grams
Percentage of calories from fat: 23%

BUTTERSCOTCH PUDDING

2 c. low-fat (1%) milk
3 Tbsp. cornstarch
⅓ c. packed dark brown
   sugar
¼ c. reconstituted butter-
   flavored mix
½ tsp. vanilla
¼ tsp. rum extract

In a medium bowl, whisk the milk and cornstarch until smooth; set aside. In a 3 quart saucepan over medium heat, heat the brown sugar and butter-flavored mix, stirring, until the mixture begins to boil. Stir in the milk mixture; bring to a boil. Boil 2 minutes, stirring constantly.

Remove the saucepan from the heat; stir in the vanilla and rum extract. Pour the pudding into four 6 ounce custard cups. Cover and refrigerate 3 hours or until chilled. Makes 4 servings.

Per serving:
Calories: 151
Fat: 1 gram
Percentage of calories from fat: 8%

CHERRY CHEESECAKE DELIGHT

Crust:
2 c. crushed fat-free
   cinnamon crackers
   (about 1½ boxes)
3 Tbsp. sugar
3 to 4 Tbsp. liquid butter
   substitute

Filling:
8 oz. fat-free cream
   cheese
½ c. sugar
2 egg substitute (½ c.)
1 tsp. lemon juice
1 tsp. vanilla
3 Tbsp. flour

Topping:
1 (21 oz.) can cherry pie
   filling (regular)
1 (1.3 oz.) pkg. prepared
   whipped topping mix (2
   c.)
2 Tbsp. whole grain
   cereal

Press the graham cracker mixture, after well blended, into the bottom of a 9½ x 13 inch casserole dish that has been sprayed with non-fat cooking spray. Beat all the filling ingredients together until smooth. Bake in 350°F. oven for 20 to 30 minutes. Insert knife to see it if comes out clean. Cool. Spread cherry pie filling over top. Top with low-fat whipped topping. Makes 24 servings.

Per serving:
Calories: 113
Fat: 1 gram
Percentage of calories from fat: 7%

CHERRY-ALMOND TORTE

1 pkg. white angel food
   cake mix
½ tsp. almond extract
1 c. marshmallow creme
1 (21 oz.) can cherry pie
   filling
¼ c. sliced almonds,
   toasted

Prepare cake mix as directed on package, except add almond extract with the water. Pour into pan. Bake and cool as directed. Remove from pan. Split cake to make 2 layers. (To split, mark side of cake with toothpicks and cut with long serrated knife.) Place bottom layer on serving plate. Spoon ⅔ cup of the marshmallow creme by heaping teaspoonfuls onto bottom layer. Spoon 1 cup of the pie filling between spoonfuls of marshmallow creme. Sprinkle with half of the almonds. Place other layer on top. Spoon remaining marshmallow creme and pie filling on top of cake, allowing pie filling to drizzle down sides. Sprinkle with remaining almonds. Refrigerate any remaining dessert. Makes 12 servings.

Per serving:
Calories: 254
Fat: 1 gram
Percentage of calories from fat: 5%

CHOCOLATE CREAM PIE

¾ c. sugar
⅓ c. cornstarch
6 Tbsp. cocoa
2 Tbsp. liquid butter
　substitute
½ tsp. lite salt (optional)
2½ c. skim milk
½ c. egg substitute
½ tsp. vanilla extract
9 inch baked pastry pie
　crust

Topping:
1 (1.3 oz.) env. whipped
　topping
½ c. skim milk
1 tsp. vanilla

In the top of a double boiler, combine sugar, cornstarch, liquid butter substitute, and lite salt. Mix well. Gradually stir in skim milk. Cook over boiling water, stirring, until mixture is thickened (about 10 minutes). Gradually stir half the hot mixture with the egg substitute; return to the double boiler. Cook over boiling water, stirring occasionally, 5 minutes. Remove from heat. Stir in vanilla. Pour chocolate filling into baked pie shell. Refrigerate 3 hours, or until well chilled. Top with 1 package whipped topping mix prepared with skim milk and vanilla. Serve immediately. Makes 8 servings.

Per serving:
Calories: 294
Fat: 10 grams
Percentage of calories from fat: 30%

HOMEMADE ICE CREAM

1½ c. evaporated
　skimmed milk
1 large egg or ¼ c. egg
　substitute
4 medium bananas,
　mashed
1½ tsp. vanilla extract
Sugar substitute to equal
　½ c. sugar (12 packets)
½ c. low-fat (1%) milk

In 5 cup ice cream maker, combine all ingredients, except milk. Add milk to bring mixture up to fill line. (Add more milk if necessary.) Freeze according to manufacturer's directions. Makes 8 servings.

Per serving:
Calories: 114
Fat: 1 gram
Percentage of calories from fat: 9%

MOCHA PUDDING

1½ oz. unsweetened
   chocolate
2½ c. low-fat milk
½ c. double-strength
   coffee
¼ c. cornstarch
¾ c. sugar
⅛ tsp. salt
3 Tbsp. half & half

Place the chocolate in a 2 quart glass bowl and cook it on MEDIUM (50% power) for 2 to 3 minutes. (Though the chocolate will appear not to have melted, it will be soft.) Whisk the milk and coffee into the chocolate. Combine the cornstarch, sugar, and salt; whisk them into the milk mixture. Microwave the contents of the bowl on HIGH for 4 minutes. Whisk the mixture and continue cooking it on HIGH, whisking every 60 seconds, until it thickens, 4 to 6 minutes more. Pour the pudding into 6 dessert cups and refrigerate them for at least 1 hour. Just before serving the pudding, dribble ½ tablespoon of the half & half over each portion. Makes 6 servings.

Per serving:
Calories: 221
Fat: 6 grams
Percentage of calories from fat: 23%

PEACH CRISP

Cooking spray
7 large peaches
2 to 3 Tbsp. lemon juice
1 tsp. grated lemon zest
Several gratings nutmeg
2 Tbsp. unsalted butter
⅔ c. sifted all-purpose
   flour
½ c. rolled oats
⅔ c. tightly packed light
   brown sugar

Preheat to oven to 325°F. Spray a 9x9 inch ovenproof dish with cooking spray. Fill up a small pot with water and put it on to boil. Dip each peach in the water for 30 seconds, then peel it and remove the pit. Slice the peaches thinly and put the slices in the prepared dish. Sprinkle with the lemon juice, grated zest, and nutmeg; toss gently.

Cut the butter into 5 or 6 pieces and put these in a bowl with the flour, oats, and brown sugar. Mix together, using a pastry blender or 2 knives. When crumbly, spoon the topping over the peaches, trying to cover them evenly. Bake for 30 minutes, or until the peaches are tender. If you would like the top to be a little browner, run the dish under the broiler for 40 seconds or so and watch constantly. Serve at room temperature. Makes 6 servings.

Per serving:
Calories: 255
Fat: 5 grams
Percentage of calories from fat: 16%

PUMPKIN CUSTARD

¼ c. packed brown sugar
½ tsp. ground cinnamon
¼ tsp. ground nutmeg
½ tsp. salt
1 egg, beaten
1 c. canned pumpkin
⅔ c. evaporated skim
   milk

Preheat oven to 350°. Lightly oil four 6 ounce custard cups. Mix sugar, cinnamon, nutmeg, and salt together in medium bowl. Add egg and mix to blend ingredients. Add pumpkin and milk; stir to combine. Pour into cups and place in a shallow pan of hot water. Bake 45 minutes or until knife comes out clean. Makes 4 servings.

Per serving:
Calories: 127
Fat: 2 grams
Percentage of calories from fat: 11%

PUMPKIN PIE

9 inch unbaked pie shell
½ c. firmly packed brown
   sugar
1 tsp. ground cinnamon
1 tsp. ground ginger
¼ tsp. ground nutmeg
Pinch of ground cloves
1 (16 oz.) can pumpkin
   puree
1¼ c. evaporated skim
   milk
3 large egg whites

Preheat oven to 350°F. Bake pie crust until lightly browned, about 10 minutes. Remove from oven and let cool to room temperature. Preheat oven to 450°F.

In a large bowl, beat all filling ingredients until no lumps remain. Pour into pie shell and bake 10 minutes. Reduce heat to 325°F. and bake 50 minutes more, or until a knife inserted in the center comes out clean. Makes 8 servings.

Per serving:
Calories: 219
Fat: 7 grams
Percentage of calories from fat: 29%

FROZEN RASPBERRY BROWNIE DESSERT

1 (20 oz.) pkg. light fudge
   brownie mix
Vegetable cooking spray
4 c. raspberry low-fat
   frozen yogurt, softened
½ c. chocolate graham
   snacks crumbs (about
   44 cookies)
2 c. fresh raspberries

Prepare brownie mix according to package directions, using a 13x9x2 inch baking pan coated with cooking spray. Bake at 350° for 20 minutes. Cool completely. Spread softened yogurt evenly over cooled brownies. Sprinkle crumbs over yogurt; cover and freeze 5 hours or until firm.

To serve, cut brownies into bars and top each bar with raspberries. Makes 16 (1 bar plus 2 tablespoons raspberries).

Per serving:
Calories: 214
Fat: 3 grams
Percentage of calories from fat: 14%

RASPBERRY YOGURT SMOOTHIE

½ c. fresh or frozen
    raspberries, thawed
1 Tbsp. sugar
¾ c. skim milk
8 oz. ctn. lemon yogurt

In blender container, combine raspberries and sugar. Cover; blend until raspberries are crushed. Add milk and yogurt; blend until smooth. Serve immediately. Makes 2 servings.

Per serving:
Calories: 190
Fat: 2 grams
Percentage of calories from fat: 7%

STRAWBERRY PIE

¾ c. all-purpose flour
¼ tsp. salt
2 Tbsp. plus 2 tsp.
    margarine, well chilled
¼ c. plain nonfat yogurt
4 c. strawberries, halved
¼ c. plus 2 Tbsp.
    granulated sugar
3 Tbsp. cornstarch
½ c. whipped topping

To prepare crust, in medium bowl, stir together flour and salt; using pastry blender or 2 knives, cut in margarine until mixture resembles coarse meal. Quickly stir in yogurt and 1 tablespoon water. Form dough into a ball, cover with plastic wrap, and refrigerate 1 hour. Preheat oven to 400°F.

Roll pastry between 2 sheets of wax paper into 9 inch circle. Fit into 9 inch pie plate; prick with fork. Line crust with aluminum foil; fill with dried beans or pie weights. Bake 15 to 18 minutes, until golden brown. Remove foil and beans; cool on rack.

To prepare filling, place 1 cup strawberries and ⅔ cup water in 2 quart saucepan; cook over medium heat for 2 minutes. In small bowl, combine sugar, cornstarch, and ⅓ cup water; add to strawberry mixture and cook until mixture boils and thickens, about 1 minute.

Reserve 8 strawberry halves for garnish. Place remaining berries in cooled pie crust; pour cooked strawberry mixture over top. Refrigerate, uncovered, until filling is completely cool, about 1 hour.

Using pastry bag fitted with star tip, decoratively pipe whipped topping onto pie. Garnish with reserved strawberry halves. Makes 8 servings.

Per serving:
Calories: 168
Fat: 5 grams
Percentage of calories from fat: 27%

STRAWBERRY YOGURT FREEZE

16 oz. nonfat strawberry
  yogurt
1 pt. strawberries, hulled
1 tsp. grated orange peel
  (optional)

Spoon the yogurt into an ice cube tray and place in the freezer until the yogurt is frozen, 3 to 4 hours. Remove the yogurt cubes from the tray, place them in a food processor, and finely chop them. Add the strawberries and orange peel if desired. Process just until smooth. Serve immediately or place in the freezer and stir occasionally until firm enough to scoop, 1 to 2 hours. Makes 6 servings.

Per serving:
Calories: 92
Fat: 1 gram
Percentage of calories from fat: 9%

WATERMELON SORBET

½ c. granulated sugar
½ c. light corn syrup
½ c. water
2 Tbsp. lemon juice
9 lb. watermelon or 2 qt.
  watermelon cubes,
  seeded

Optional garnishes:
Strawberries, mint leaves

Prepare sorbet: In small saucepan over medium heat, combine sugar, corn syrup, and water; cook, stirring, until mixture boils. Boil 5 minutes without stirring. Stir in lemon juice; cool to room temperature. In blender, food processor or food mill, puree seeded watermelon. Add cooled syrup; puree until blended.

Electric or manual ice cream maker: Pour sorbet mixture into freezer can and freeze according to manufacturer's directions. If sorbet is still soft after churning, remove dasher and using large spoon, pack down in container; cover with foil and container lid. Return to machine; pack with ice or place in freezer about 2 to 3 hours before serving.

Freezer method: Pour sorbet mixture into 9 inch square baking pan; cover with foil or plastic wrap and place in freezer, stirring once, until frozen around edges but still slushy in center, 1 to 3 hours (depending on freezer temperature). Spoon into large bowl; with mixer at medium speed, beat until smooth but still frozen. Return sorbet to pan; cover and freeze until firm. Makes 1 quart (8 servings).

Party sorbet balls: Prescooped sorbet will slow melting. Into shallow baking pan lined with waxed paper, arrange scoops of sorbet in single layer. Cover with foil or plastic wrap; freeze until serving time. Arrange scoops in chilled serving bowl; garnish as desired.

Per serving:
Calories: 166
Fat: 1 gram
Percentage of calories from fat: 3%

MISCELLANEOUS

COCKTAIL SAUCE

12 oz. chili sauce
  (homemade or bought)
1 Tbsp. horseradish
  (prepared)
1 Tbsp. lemon juice
½ tsp. Worcestershire
  sauce
Pinch of salt
Dash of pepper

Mix all ingredients. Cover and refrigerate any leftover sauce.

Per recipe:
Calories: 397
Fat: 0 gram
Percentage of calories from fat: 0%

BBQ SAUCE

½ c. tomato puree
¼ c. vinegar
¼ c. minced onion
2 Tbsp. Worcestershire
  sauce
1 pack artificial sweetener
¼ tsp. dry mustard
Garlic powder

Heat all ingredients to boiling over medium heat, stirring constantly. Reduce heat. Simmer, uncovered, stirring occasionally, 15 minutes.

Per recipe:
Calories: 105
Fat: Less than 1 gram
Percentage of calories from fat: 5%

BREAKFAST PARFAITS

1 c. quick-cooking or old-
  fashioned oats
  (uncooked)
2 (8 oz.) containers
  vanilla nonfat yogurt
1 (8 oz.) can crushed
  pineapple in juice
  (undrained)
2 Tbsp. sliced almonds
  (optional)
2 c. sliced fresh or
  thawed frozen
  strawberries

In medium bowl, combine oats, yogurt, pineapple, and almonds; mix well. Cover; refrigerate overnight or up to 1 week. To serve, layer oat mixture and strawberries into 4 parfait glasses. Garnish with additional strawberries. Serve chilled. Makes 4 servings.

Note: You may substitute 1 cup uncooked multigrain oatmeal for oats.

Per serving:
Calories: 252
Fat: 4 grams
Percentage of calories from fat: 13%

CHICKEN STOCK

3 lb. chicken, skinned and
  all visible fat removed
3 qt. water
1 medium onion, coarsely
  chopped
2 stalks celery, chopped
2 large carrots, chopped
1 tsp. whole peppercorns
  or to taste
½ inch piece peeled, fresh
  ginger, chopped
  (optional)
1 bay leaf
1 tsp. dried thyme

In a large stockpot, bring all ingredients to a boil over medium-high heat. Reduce heat and simmer, partially covered, for at least 1 hour, or until chicken is tender. Frequently skim the froth off the top. Remove chicken and strain stock. (The chicken meat can be used in salads.)

To defat stock, refrigerate until the fat hardens on the surface, then remove and discard. The stock may gel during refrigeration; this is natural. Makes 2½ quarts.

Per serving:
Calories: 14
Fat: Less than 1 gram
Percentage of calories from fat: 13%

FLORENTINE SAUCE FOR PASTA

2 lb. fresh spinach
2 Tbsp. liquid butter
  substitute
3 Tbsp. flour
2 c. skim milk
1 tsp. lite salt (optional)
1¾ c. nonfat cottage
  cheese (or nonfat
  Ricotta cheese)
¼ c. fat-free Parmesan
  cheese

Carefully wash spinach and break off tough ends. Chop spinach leaves, then steam for 2 to 3 minutes. Drain well, pressing through sieve or colander to make sure all water is removed; set aside. In top of a double boiler over boiling water, heat liquid butter substitute. Add flour, stirring constantly for about 2 to 3 minutes. Add milk, a little at a time, stirring constantly with a wire whisk. Add the lite salt and continue to stir until sauce thickens, about 10 minutes. Add all the other ingredients, including drained spinach. Mix thoroughly and heat through. Serve over the pasta of your choice. Makes 12 servings.

Per serving:
Calories: 62
Fat: Less than 1 gram
Percentage of calories from fat: 6%

GRAVY

1 c. fat free chicken broth
3 Tbsp. instant nonfat dry milk
1 Tbsp. all-purpose flour
1/2 tsp. chicken flavored bouillon granules
1/2 c. water
1/2 tsp. browning and seasoning sauce

Place broth in small saucepan. Add dry milk and remaining ingredients. Bring to a boil; reduce heat and simmer for 5 minutes, stirring frequently. Makes 8 servings.

Per serving:
Calories per 3 tablespoons: 16
Fat: Less than 1 gram
Percentage of calories from fat: 6%

QUICK CREAMY ALFREDO SAUCE

1 c. evaporated skim milk
1/4 c. liquid butter substitute
1/4 c. flour
4 tsp. fat-free chicken broth
1/4 c. fat-free Parmesan cheese
1/4 tsp. minced garlic (in a jar)
1/4 tsp. ground pepper
1/4 tsp. lite salt (optional)

In a small saucepan over low heat, blend flour, liquid butter substitute, skim milk, and chicken broth. Add minced garlic, salt, and pepper. Continue to cook over low heat until the sauce thickens. Stir in Parmesan cheese and serve immediately. Serve with cooked fettuccine (10 to 12 ounces, cooked). Makes 6 servings.

Note: You can make a delicious entree with this sauce by adding 4 chopped cooked skinless chicken breasts and an 8 ounce can sliced mushrooms, drained.

Per serving:
Calories: 66
Fat: Less than 1 gram
Percentage of calories from fat: 1%

SEASONING BLEND

2 Tbsp. leaf oregano
2 Tbsp. parsley flakes
4 tsp. sweet leaf basil
4 tsp. leaf tarragon
4 Tbsp. onion powder
1 tsp. leaf sage
4 Tbsp. garlic powder
2 tsp. ground marjoram
1 1/2 tsp. ground black pepper
1/2 tsp. ground thyme

In bowl, combine oregano, parsley flakes, basil, tarragon, and sage. Crush with fingers until fine. Stir in onion powder, garlic powder, marjoram, pepper, and thyme until blended. Spoon into shaker.

Use to season meat, chicken, fish, casseroles, salads, and vegetables.

Per recipe:
Calories: 258
Fat: 2 grams
Percentage of calories from fat: 6%

MOCK SOUR CREAM

1 c. low-fat cottage
  cheese
2 Tbsp. skim milk
1 Tbsp. lemon juice

Puree the cottage cheese in a blender, about 2 minutes, and thin to desired consistency with the skim milk and the lemon juice. Makes 16 servings (1 cup total).

Per serving:
Calories per 1 tablespoon: 11
Fat: Less than 1 gram
Percentage of calories from fat: 17%

SEASONED BREAD CRUMBS

4 slices whole wheat
  bread
1 Tbsp. dried parsley
  flakes
1/2 tsp. dried basil
1/2 tsp. dried oregano
1 Tbsp. dried onion flakes
1/4 c. grated Parmesan
  cheese

Preheat oven to 275°F. Arrange bread slices in a single layer on a baking sheet. Bake 15 to 20 minutes, or until crisp and dry. Break slices into pieces and reduce to crumbs, using a blender or a food processor, or by placing bread pieces in a plastic bag and crushing with a rolling pin. Add remaining ingredients and stir to mix well. Store refrigerated in an airtight container. Makes 16 servings.

Per serving:
Calories: 24
Fat: 1 gram
Percentage of calories from fat: 24%

TOMATO SALAD DRESSING

1 (8 oz.) can tomato
  sauce
1 tsp. Worcestershire
  sauce
1/2 tsp. dried basil,
  crushed
2 Tbsp. tarragon vinegar
1/2 tsp. dried dill weed
1/2 tsp. onion juice

In screw-top jar, combine tomato sauce, tarragon, vinegar, Worcestershire sauce, dried dill weed, basil, and onion juice. Cover and shake well; chill thoroughly. Shake again before serving. Makes 16 servings.

Per serving:
Calories per 1 tablespoon: 5
Fat: 0 grams
Percentage of calories from fat: 0%

INDEX OF RECIPES

APPETIZERS, BEVERAGES

BANANA SMOOTHIE 5
CHEESY PIZZA SNACKS 3
COTTAGE CHEESE SPREAD 1
CRAB TOAST APPETIZERS 3
CRAN-BANANA COOLER 5
CUCUMBER DILL DIP 1
GRANOLA 4
LAYERED MEXICAN DIP 2
ORANGE-STRAWBERRY JUICE FROTH 5
PINEAPPLE-APRICOT SPREAD 2
POTATO SKINS 4
RASPBERRY COOLER 6
SCALLOP AND HAM ROLL-UPS 4
TURKEY MEATBALLS 5
TUTTI-FRUTTI COOLER 6
VEGETABLE DIP 2
YOGURT SHAKE 6

SOUPS, SALADS

ALL-OCCASION SOUP 7
BEAN AND CABBAGE SOUP 7
BEAN AND MACARONI STEW 8
BEAN 'N' GREENS SOUP 8
CHEESY CREAMY BROCCOLI SOUP 9
CHICKEN BROTH 10
CHICKPEA AND BROWN RICE SOUP 10
CORN AND POTATO CHOWDER 11
CREAMY POTATO SALAD 18
CURRIED VEGETABLE SALAD 14
FRENCH ONION SOUP 12
HOMESTYLE TURKEY SOUP 14
LENTIL-SAUSAGE SOUP 12
MEATBALL SOUP 13
MEXICAN PASTA SALAD 17
MOCK EGG SALAD SANDWICHES 15
NEW POTATO SALAD WITH GREEN GODDESS
    DRESSING 17
ORIENTAL SALAD 18
PEA SALAD 16
QUICK BEAN-ROTINI SOUP 9
QUICK TOMATO BARLEY SOUP 13
ROAST BEEF AND PASTA SALAD 19
SEAFOOD FRUIT SALAD 15
SOUTHWEST CHICKEN SOUP 11
TACO SALAD 19
TUNA-PASTA SALAD 20
TUNA SALAD 20
TURKEY-BARLEY SOUP 14
TWENTY-FOUR HOUR SALAD 16

VEGETABLES

BAKED BEANS 21
BROCCOLI CHEESE-RICE CASSEROLE 22
COLESLAW 23
CORN-CARROT CASSEROLE 23
CREOLE LIMA BEANS 21
GLAZED CARROTS 23
HONEY-GLAZED CARROTS 24
MAC 'N CHEESE 25
MASHED POTATOES 26
MEXICAN BEAN BAKE 21
MIXED VEGETABLE PASTA 30

OVEN ROASTED POTATO WEDGES 24
REFRIED BEANS 22
ROSEMARY-BAKED RED POTATOES 27
SCALLOPED POTATOES 25
STEAMED NEW POTATOES WITH GARLIC
    SAUCE 26
STUFFED SWEET POTATOES 28
TOMATO AND BROCCOLI CASSEROLE 29
TWICE-BAKED POTATOES 27
VEGETABLE FRIED RICE 28

MAIN DISHES

BAKED CHICKEN BREASTS 34
BARBECUED CHICKEN 34
BROCCOLI LASAGNA 50
BROILED SAGE CHICKEN 35
CAJUN CHICKEN WITH BEANS AND
    RICE 35
CHICKEN-BASIL NOODLES 36
CHICKEN CHILI ENCHILADAS 37
CHICKEN DIVAN 37
CHICKEN FETTUCCINE 38
CHICKEN GYROS 38
CHICKEN SPAGHETTI 39
CHILES RELLENOS CASSEROLE 50
CHILI CHICKEN 36
COD FILLETS WITH VEGETABLES 45
DIJON CHICKEN BREASTS 41
EASY SAUSAGE BALLS 47
FAJITAS WITH PICO DE GALLO 31
FETTUCCINE WITH TOMATO SAUCE 51
FETTUCINI WITH FRESH HERBS 51
GINGER CHICKEN STIR-FRY 39
GRILLED ROUND STEAK WITH TOMATILLO
    SAUCE 32
HAWAIIAN PIZZA 44
HOT HAM SANDWICHES 43
ITALIAN CASSEROLE 52
LEMONY CHICKEN 40
MACARONI AND CHEESE 52
MARINATED COCKTAIL MEATBALLS 32
MEXICAN BAKED FISH 45
MEXICAN LASAGNA 48
MEXICAN SPAGHETTI 40
OPEN-FACE ROAST BEEF SANDWICHES 33
ORIENTAL BARBECUED CHICKEN 41
PASTA WITH GARLIC AND HERBS 53
PITA TACOS 53
PORK AND BARLEY SKILLET SUPPER 44
REUBEN SANDWICHES 48
ROAST BEEF HASH 33
SEAFOOD-STUFFED PEPPERS 46
SKILLET CHICKEN 42
SOUTHWEST SCRAMBLED EGGS 54
SPANISH CHICKEN WITH RICE 43
SPICY CHICKEN 42
STUFFED CHICKEN BREAST 43
TUNA NOODLE CASSEROLE 46
TUNA PITA 47
TURKEY MEATBALL STROGANOFF 49
TURKEY POCKETS 49
VEGETARIAN HOT DISH 54

BREADS, ROLLS

APPLE-RAISIN SPICE BREAD 55
BANANA SPICE BREAD 55
CORN BREAD. 56
CORN BREAD DRESSING 59
CORN PANCAKES. 59
FRENCH TOAST 59
FRUITY MUFFINS 57
GERMAN APPLE PANCAKE. 60
OAT AND RAISIN BRAN MUFFINS 58
ORANGE CHOCOLATE CHIP BREAD. 56
PANCAKES. 60
PUMPKIN MUFFINS. 58
STRAWBERRY BREAD 57

DESSERTS

APPLE CRISP 66
BAKLAVA 67
BANANA SPLIT DESSERT 68
BASIC GRAHAM CRACKER CRUST 65
BLUEBERRY COFFEE CAKE 62
BLUEBERRY-PEACH CRUMBLE. 68
BLUEBERRY UPSIDE-DOWN CAKE 62
BREAD PUDDING 69
BROWNIES. 70
BUTTERSCOTCH PUDDING. 70
CARROT CAKE WITH VANILLA SAUCE. 63
CHERRY-ALMOND TORTE. 71
CHERRY CHEESECAKE DELIGHT 71
CHOCOLATE CAKE 63

CHOCOLATE CREAM PIE 72
FRESH BLUEBERRY PIE 69
FRESH LEMON COOKIES 65
FROZEN BANANA DESSERT CUPS 67
FROZEN RASPBERRY BROWNIE
    DESSERT 74
FRUIT-TOPPED ANGEL FOOD CAKE 61
HOMEMADE ICE CREAM 72
HOT FUDGE PUDDING CAKE 64
MOCHA PUDDING 73
PASTRY PIE CRUST 66
PEACH CRISP. 73
PUMPKIN CUSTARD 74
PUMPKIN PIE 74
RASPBERRY YOGURT SMOOTHIE 75
7 MINUTE FAT-FREE FROSTING 64
STRAWBERRY PIE 75
STRAWBERRY YOGURT FREEZE. 76
WATERMELON SORBET 76

MISCELLANEOUS

BBQ SAUCE 77
BREAKFAST PARFAITS 77
CHICKEN STOCK 78
COCKTAIL SAUCE 77
FLORENTINE SAUCE FOR PASTA 78
GRAVY. 79
MOCK SOUR CREAM 80
QUICK CREAMY ALFREDO SAUCE. 79
SEASONED BREAD CRUMBS 80
SEASONING BLEND 79
TOMATO SALAD DRESSING 80